Therein Goodness Stands You

by

Pauly Boy

DORRANCE PUBLISHING CO., INC.
PITTSBURGH, PENNSYLVANIA 15222

For more information or to order additional books, please write:
Dorrance Publishing Co., Inc.
643 Smithfield Street
Pittsburgh, Pennsylvania 15222
U.S.A.

This book is dedicated to my family and friends:

    For my friends who may not know me as well as my family, my truthful testimony, as well as other moral-related topics before my introduction, which sets the tone for my work.

    You will find four very important things of worth throughout this book, "truth, love, virtue and compassion." We can't walk around without these gifts in our heart. All of these characters together will bring us closer to ourselves, Jesus and our heavenly Father. It's your choice to win or lose, there's nothing more I can do, other than reveal the true side of a few of God's gifts and goal for you.

    I've produced a mixed blend of secular and religious pieces of workmanship which I hope people will one day realize; each side needs the other to survive.

    There is an afterword at the end of my book, and it is my hope that something will reach you in a powerful way causing you to go out and help keep the world alive, while we wait for the truth from on high to set us free.

A Special Message

To those very meaningful, kind, God-seeking brothers, sisters, and their children too, everything in this book is just for you. On the other hand, I realize there's no way possible to please everyone. However, there will be people who might feel slighted in some way and try to downgrade my work. All I can say is: "Remember, we were all put here for a purpose and no one knows why, or for how long, until it's made known through time." I feel as though I've practiced what I preached after becoming born again. This is the way I spell "reality,": (Jehovah God, Jesus Christ and the Holy Ghost).

People would say I'm a mongrel of sorts, as I have four different nationalities which are English, Indian, Irish and Scottish (alphabetically).

Off the record here, these are the first few pieces of poetry that I have put together. I wrote; Looking At You, Hoping To Share A Feeling, Divided, He Will Always Ride Free, The Way Out, Our Father and Let's Journey Together.

I worked at different jobs for awhile until I found myself employed in the metal trades as a welder from November of 1973 to May of 1990.

I wish to give special thanks to Mr. Ray Ellis of New London, Connecticut who gave me the idea for my style of writing, which I will always use. I love u brother Ray.

I would very much like to give thanks to Mr. Bill W. Johnson of Houston, Texas for doing all the editing work in my book. I love you, Billy, and thanks brother, it meant a lot to me really.

I would like to extend a very warm welcome to brother Charlie Sherbert of New London, Connecticut whose last piece of poetry in my book is because of him. He wrote it and I helped put it together years ago. I told him if I ever put a book together I would add it as an honorable mention. It tells a true story of how men and women are today and the mistakes they make without God in their lives. I love ya Charlie, and I'll miss u dude.

Special Thanks:

All Spelling Is Intentional

    I would like to give special thanks to my family and friends, and you know who you are. Even though our lives were like riding the ol' rollercoaster, I love you all very much. One day when we're all together again and it's not too far away, this happiness we've been looking for will be there for real and for the other families too, who are seeking and doing the truth for everyone concerned.

    I would like to give special thanks to a couple of great families and places: Mr. Jim and Lillian Smith and their family of New London, Connecticut; Mr. Musser and Betty Bohn and their family of Frazier, Pennsylvania; Mr. John Hashem's Pizza Place in Frazier, Pennsylvania, where he makes the best double cheese steak grinders with mayo in the "swivelized world!" (smile). I loved all of you more than words could ever express. I would like to give special thanks to all those brothers and sisters I never got to meet, though tomorrow is another day. May peace be with you. I would like to give special thanks to the following people who stand out in my thoughts, as they shaped my life at a young age while in the military service.

    U.S.A.F. Major Van Bibber Schweinfurt, Germany 1969 -1971. He was a brother who loved his two sons and the Boy Scouts of good ol' Troop 55. He taught me how to reach the children. Yeah, that Klondike Derby was awesome. I'm missin' u and your boys.

    U.S. Army Captain Charles Badgett (chuck-smile) H.H.C. 3rd Inf. Div. Schweinfurt, Germany 1969-1971. Charles helped me through the years understanding the changes that were affecting me, as well as the rest of the brothers for whom he was responsible. At the time he probably didn't know it, but he made me see things about the races of people like the minority groups of Black, Spanish speaking and Indian people, who I feel for most of all. Though you try making things right within the races, yet none of us seem to fit in (one another's space) no matter where we are or what we try to do. It's like everyone always thinks the worst and we can never reach one another. I wish it wasn't that way. When I left Germany I knew I had to do something right, and thanks to the brothers in the message center and everyone in my unit at our H.H.C and especially you Charles, I was able to find my answers over the years. Since I realized what freedom means, though it was a while later, "that truth and freedom for someone who is suppose to be, but really isn't, is why we're where we are today; caught up in the sufferings of an unjust world!" You to me Charles, I can't forget. I love u buddy.

    A very special thanks goes out to Mr. George Hendry, his wife Pauline (my little buddy) of Waterford, Connecticut. George is an honest landlord who cared for his tenants.

(B)

If there were more landlords like him there wouldn't be a need for rent control. I wish you both the very best in life always.

Special mention indeed goes out to an ol' friend, Alexander Rocholl of Schweinfurt, Germany and his family members, especially his sister Annette. I miss ya'zz. Hope all is well with everyone there. I've not forgotten any of you and never will. We'll see each other again and pig out on some of that awesome German ice-cream. You didn't think I forgot u now did ya? (smile)

Now, how could I ever forget my main wheel man, Mr. Jimmy Da Mato of Enfield, CT? Yeah, we've cruised up and down the highways a few times in that ol' Buick of yours. Kinda made me think of the space shuttle a little bit. I swear if that baby had wings I know it could fly brother. (smile) Give my best to your wife and children. Remember, I love an' miss ya more than u know man.

Last but not least, I would like to express special thanks, going out to Mr. Jimmy Michael and Mr. Timmy Di Vita, from New London, Connecticut. I've known them since Jump Street and I'm wishin' both of you and your families my best always. I love u guys like a "FATMAN," so let's rock on together because "the blues I love and I rock to roll," yeah, it still holds the magic sound. (smile)

My personal thoughts about my work:

"It isn't much but It's all I've got to give. I just <u>hope</u> it's enough."

Romans: Chap. 15 Vrs. 13
Check it out sometime

(C)

My Testimony

When I grew up at the age of 17 years old, I left Montville High School in my native Connecticut and enlisted into the U.S. Army in 1968. I served three years overseas in Germany, and my discharge date out of country back to America was in July of 1971. In 1972 I was living and working over on Fishers Island, New York, where early one afternoon I sat alone on the floor of my living room. In thought about life, I looked up at the wall where I saw this huge purple-spaded flower. It covered eight feet in height and seven feet across in width. There were colors moving around throughout the inside of this beautiful vision, like the inner workings of an engine motor. I know one day we'll all see the reason why. I didn't realize until years later what the vision meant. It was clearly a sign that, God Almighty our Father in heaven is the "Trump of life," who holds all power and wisdom throughout the universe, which He Himself created.

I decided later to go overseas again around November, 1972 to Ascension Island, which is located off the southern coast of South Africa. While there, I was working a lot when I had my biggest encounter spiritually concerning God's plan for my life. I was working twelve-hour shifts for a while and when I came off shift early one morning I ate at the cafeteria and told my roommate I was crashing out and locking the door so he wouldn't disturb me. He said, "No problem, because I'm going someplace else today." I left the cafeteria and went to my room and locked the door, took a shower and went to bed about ten o'clock, the morning of March 22, 1973.

I was awakened later by something pressing on the back of my neck and as I tried to roll over from off my stomach to see who was messing around with me, I realized I was totally alone, paralyzed and could not move a muscle. I got scared because I was thinking that I had just gone to bed a few hours ago and I was healthy as could be. I wasn't saved at the time so you could imagine I had a few choice words for the situation in which I found myself. Though no matter how much I tried struggling and cursing to myself, nothing I did changed the fix I was in. All of a sudden the room started to turn dark and I really started to freak out because I felt for the first time in my life like I was going to buy the farm, (die). Just then these thoughts came rushing through my head, like what purpose is there for this world anyway. Or why was I here in the first place. I didn't even know anything about the truth in life, or why this was happening to me now. As these thoughts scrambled through my brain at light speed, I could see the room was getting darker to the point where all the light was fading quickly. Seconds later, the room was in total darkness and a big black hole or sphere formed up near my face as I could see it in the darkness. Right then my spirit came out from between my eyes and started falling downward fast into the darkness and I

(D)

knew this was it, as I could feel and sense death gripping me, so I screamed out inside my head and said, "If there's a God please help me!" That split second I could feel a force rush through the back of my head and go down into the darkness and retrieve my spirit, bringing it back up replacing it again, between my eyes. Instantly I was released, rolling over and sitting up in my bed, shaking, crying and in a drenching cold sweat, thanking God, Jesus and the Holy Ghost for saving my worthless non-believing life. I knew at that moment for the first time in my life there really was an' invisible, all knowing, loving, powerful Almighty God in heaven who holds the keys to life and death! Praise be to God, Jesus Christ His Son, and the Holy Ghost. As I sat up in my bed something came into my body ever so gently, sharing those secrets I was longing for in my head when the ordeal was going on. I knew there was a Creator of life, and me a somebody. This loving God created a very special Son, His only Son in Jesus Christ and the Holy Ghost, which is the sacred Trinity eternally. I knew Jesus came to earth and was in fact crucified on the cross for my sins and the sins of the world. He truly is the "Lamb of God," the one we must respect and come to know and love in our lives. The vile evil darkness I felt closed in and tried to kill me, made me burn with hate for the devil, like a red-hot cinder I know will never fizzle out! For he is my Father's enemy and he is mine too, for what he has done and will do to the children and our people of this earth!

I then managed to crawl out of bed and make it over to my desk and chair, where I started to write down on paper a bunch of words that were jumping out of my head for about forty-five minutes straight. I just sat there looking at these words for a few hours until I realized I had to go back to work, in the material world once again. Needless to say I was a basket case all that night. When I got off shift the next day I went down to the seashore and let the sea breeze flow over me as I kept reworking those words I had written the day before, thinking how good it was to be alive and having a second chance at life. Before I left Ascension Island I had formed those words into my first two pieces of poetry, which I felt explained what I wanted to do or I hoped God wanted me to do for Him. After the next four years that followed and the hardships I endured, I started to realize God was giving me things spiritually to write down, helping in the fight to free His children, "bringing them into the light of salvation," His world and love forever.

Over the years I've given away many free copies of my manuscript and single pieces in hopes of finding some feedback. The idea Christians and non-Christians seem to get from reading my work is, "Poor Paul, his life is so sad." No, let me say it's not about me, it's about you and the people next door throughout the world, as it will come to pass. In reality many people have not been touched by God in the way others have, for them to realize the true spiritual stage of things to come because it hasn't manifested itself in their walk as yet. When it does, they will say, "Yeah, it makes sense now, for one can not know to feel the sorrow until it hits (you) like a hammer; as that person will know then the truth of what is written." There are different levels of plains we seek to reach and God does grant them when He sees that we can handle what He gives us, "as it takes a broken vessel to help a broken vessel." Unless God grants you what is needed at that moment to heal your surrounding situation without putting you through the spiritual war, there will be suffering torment in the trials an tribulations of your journey called life. For some, our burden is heavier and lasts longer than others which you might be enduring now. Whether you believe or not, nobody's exempt from the hurt and pain. Some have to carry a little more than others because they can deal with it, as we are to lead by example. When things aren't going well, you may secretly blame God for your problems, but let me share with ya what I've found. The evil one comes into everybody's life sooner or later and works through us spiritually until he hears that person blaming God because he can't get a healing or a domestic problem solved when he wants it right away. Maybe that person doesn't know God's Word too well or doesn't believe in any type of healing through His anointed ones. And no, we don't know why God might allow a situation to linger for awhile, but put the blame where it truly belongs. No, don't blame God, blame the devil for your grief, then take a good long hard look at yourself!

To the right extreme however, this may tickle your funny bone and you just might laugh yourself silly, but let me reinforce one thing in your carnal mind. Life isn't just a one way ticket, you're here, then you're gone, that's it, the end, see ya later, bye. In this world we have those people who believe in a "higher power somewhere," which the unsaved soul doesn't want to admit, "it's God all along who pulled them through because then they'd have to submit." The story is told of two monks out in some remote place in the ozone, who got drunk one night and one said to the other, "Hey, let's write a book and call it the Bible so men will be able to choose between a good guy and a bad guy. We'll call the good guy a living eternal God of all creation and the bad guy His enemy, a dark evil deceiver, the devil. That way we will have some kind of civil order that will keep us from destroying ourselves if we can fool'em, lest we bring the wrath of death on all our heads." Then the other monk said, "Yeah, that's the ticket man, and if they're good during their life we'll reward the people by telling them they'll go to heaven, yeah that's it heaven, you know a paradise when they die here, their spirit will fly away to a better place." "Oh man," I can't believe you just said that. Wow, that's totally radical, like fifteenth dimensional dude," as both monks fell down toasted to the max and passed out from the alcohol they consumed during their dizzy hairbrain scheme.

After waking up they went to work, wrote the Bible and distributed it around to where everyone has his own version no matter how bizarre, concerning the Word of God today. No way hozay, that's not even close to the way it really is man, sorry. (smile)

Life isn't some little game we've been playing all these years. If you look around you would see our resources are almost depleted and so is, "man's morality." Something is destroying it, and this you can't even deny! If you think you've had it tough since you've been here on earth and you figure this is the real hell, remember, there's only One who's been there an back. If you leave this world without the spiritual truth of Jesus in your heart an soul, "you better know now you haven't even begun to see or feel hell, like you're gonna!" This is the truth I write about that the devil has turned into a lie, so where he goes you will follow, unless you repent of your sins and believe, changing your ways.

Don't get me wrong, there are no angels down here in this world, for many saved Christians sin too with one foot in heaven and one foot in the world, then eventually turning away from God, as many talk and profess Jesus is the way, yet they live not the life. They're backsliding, which they will pay for when they stand before the Christ, realizing only then, they're not making it in either! In the meantime, however, the saved Christian who makes the effort daily (or at least is supposed to) clearing up his problems through prayer, where the unsaved soul doesn't bother doin' anything at all except adding to the mounting heartaches that only increase until it costs him everything he's got, even his soul which is always the last thing the the devil takes. Please think about this impression I'm leaving you with so you can begin to see the changes happen, and there will be many; though the days are winding down and time is short. Hopefully you will start seeking the spiritual way because it's your unhappy ending if you choose it.

May the good Lord above bless your earthly family, if you've got one, and your search for the truth. I challenge you to look into Jesus, for He is the key to getting you out'a here alive, becoming born again. Realize, even if there's no one who knows you or loves you or understands you, Jesus does. "He is the real an only seal of authorship." Check'em out an in today, before you miss the rapture that's headed for us believers, as the hour will soon be looking you in the face no matter where you are or what you're doing. You're not going to be able to hide from the truth and power of God. Know that God cares and feels your worth is everything, and you should take the time to find out what it is, and why He is, hoping you're wanting to need Him, as well.

(G)

A Very Truthful And Personal Message

I would like you to know I'm just a person who was brought into this world like you. While I grew up I tried to find the hidden answers that will help us through the tough times ahead. We as children have the right to know the truth about our life's meaning. Through the years I felt people everywhere wanted to be free, happy and enjoy what ever type of work they do, along with helping others who were less fortunate. Today however, everyone's main concern is who can acquire the largest bank account and big business is busy "selling the working people right down the drain," as they don't care what they've got to do to get by. So they pull up their roots and move out of state and the country to maximize their profits even more! Yes it's true, the world is bought up and there isn't much left for the little working class person to have, or go visit, as it costs more than you make. I realize no one likes to be told anything (nowadays), especially if he or she isn't doing what's right, but we all learn (some of us that is) what's right at some point in time before we leave this world. It's too bad though, because it's always later than sooner for most people and the hurt they've caused, never seems to get undone no matter how much they change. People figure the world owes them or has forgotten them by taking someone close away, so instead of working for what they want they could care less what they have to do to feel good, or get by materially to gain what the next person has! If they only knew the truth they'd change in a heartbeat. When God sees favor in our work and blesses us, believe me it's the real deal.

I've listened to the brothers who came before me with truth and in time I could feel their message press into me, as I saw and sensed the world hurting. I knew something was wrong and had to be changed keeping this spirit alive, so we won't keep crumbling back into darkness. Many brothers and sisters are doing what they can. You've got to get involved in what you know you should be doing today. We've got too many couch potatoes in this crazy world. We've got to tear down those walls and let the Son shine in. Make everything in life count because the person next to you needs you and you're gonna need him or her somewhere down the road too. We are part of each other, there is no doubt. We're not going to make it without helping one another. If you don't think so, I'd hate to be the one near you when you find out the hard way!

Look, we all had the same equal chance at this spiritual favor in creation from God before we were even sent into this world, according to life's morality teaching. The brothers who hold their gifts received from God our Father are well aware of who they are, where they stand and why. Those of you who didn't fare as well as you hoped to, maybe feel let down or cheated, but God is just. It's you man, you've got to change your trip, rich or not to attain the goal, unless you're one of those silver-spoon babies, though even silver turns to rust.

(H)

Every brother will know his place in our Father's will. I'm just tellin' ya like it is. I don't expect you to believe or understand right away everything within this book though if you make the effort to read it, I know you'll find many good feelings that you will pass onto someone else, "who's searching for the truth in a cold hearted world."

Down the road you will find I wasn't one of the ones trying to deceive you or your children. As the old saying goes, "it's all going to come out in the wash." I figure if you can't see it now after all we've been through, you will, sadly enough, see it later. If you keep to yourself and away from putting any impurities into your body, the risk of problems and heartaches will be less than those who do not. Even though you will learn and keep the faith, yet you shall lose the fight, though you will win the battle against old skunk breath, (the devil) because he cannot destroy what God has made within you, as those who follow evil will find out, when they get a taste of their own poison!

I hope for you to understand more clearly the spiritual changes coming in this bleak torn world, as the news tells us more and more every passing year. Those of you who are in touch spiritually, never stop thinking about the flight from here as the power of truth and light will make your dreams become the real reality very few know of. I can't begin to tell you everything I feel or know, but I've learned "you mean more to me than you'll ever realize." You owe it to yourself to see what God has in store for the ones who love Him, Christ and the Holy Spirit. It won't be the every day boring depression with nothing to do, or that hollow feeling you get when speaking the truth to someone who professes to carry the faith, yet they're empty to submission, repentance and total belief in the living Word of Jehovah God.

I'm not trying to be anybody. I'm not preaching or lecturing to anyone. All I ever wanted in life was to be happy, free, taking care of my family, friends, and also the poor around me. My dreams never came true either to do anyone any good, but hey, there's always the lotto. (smile)

There are people out there who need a helping hand and care for the same things in life that we all were brought up believing in. This junk about hurray for me and the hell with you just doesn't cut it. People say, "God helps those who help themselves," (and I believe that's true) but I say to, "God helps those who help others first." By helping others you help yourself to understand what's happening spiritually. While waiting for the hour when we are all free and together as one, the suffering I'll carry, buried in the blues of this unrighteous world. I'll never forget or rest until we see the will of our God for ourselves, finally completed.

In closing, I wish you God's spirit of love. I love you and hope to see you all around in a twinkling of an eye. If you keep looking up, that's where the truth will be seen, unless something is goin' down with God's two witnesses here in the world when they show up. Otherwise, behold, "the Lamb of God, the redeemer of mankind cometh from above."

(I)

The Three Realms Of Knowledge

As you may or may not be aware, there are three spiritual realms within this world as we know them today. The first and most important one is heaven above.This is where many people believe there is true direction, real peace and purpose with love and joy for one another in God's Kingdom, if however our spirit is allowed to enter once we leave this world.

The second one is the lesson, in which we experience the choice of good or evil. Through these methods we have struggled to exist mostly because man cannot control the greed and suffering which should prove enough to one by now. This world is in a hold situation until the change comes to free the people who seek goodness. Like spring to winter everyone screaming they're number one in what they do best, until they are but a memory if they're lucky, "while the children continue lingering on in vain," searching for the given lesson. By this manner we hope to break evil's force-fed stream making us clean inside and out, instead of being just half whole during our time of living here.

The third and final realm is hell to come, due to the lack of respect and morality within the brothers and sisters of this world. Doing only for themselves to get by, they try to assure you that that's not true and things will be better tomorrow. They then tell you there is no hell coming, yet who knows the mind of the Father or the battle ground of the poor, the elderly, the handicapped, the starving, the abducted and abused, not to mention the homeless people. The earth is being ravaged with pollutants from the air and drinking water hardly exists in some countries. The destruction of land is an eyesore throughout the world. Our garbage is filled almost to capacity along with the nuclear-waste problem, not to mention the critical shortage of forests world wide. Let's face it, something's wrong here and the children sense it more than ever, "there's no way out for them." Who wants a world pulling at you from two different directions, pressure pushing against your brain every miserable day while you pretend everything's okay? The world is in a decaying dilemma as we watch the power of money add to the rich people's position, while the heads of state turn and look the other way, because many are on the take through some crooked scam. After getting caught, they turn and start singing like a canary on their partners, saving their own skin from doin' time up at the big house. When the dark hour comes upon you, you have been told ahead of time to become righteous within yourself, or pay dearly the price of your wrong doing!

(J)

OUR REDEEMER.

Engraved by John Rogers after the Original Painting by Guido.

The Picture:

There may be different ways people see and understand most of the things that happen to them during their walk in this world, though many never find anything because of life's busy material, money-induced schedule, which keeps it from them.

People say a picture is worth a thousand words. Yet we see it, we read and hear many words throughout our lives, though the truth never seems to reach one too fast these days, when problems need answers without delay.

If by chance the view and words express truth by which one's heart is touched fully by what he or she feels, then surely the two together make for an unforgettable experience.

This picture was shot from the book, "The Life Of Christ" of which there were only three printings done in the early to mid-18th century. From the original painting of, "Our Redeemer" produced by the famous Italian painter Guido. Being awesome an priceless to say the least, it is believed to date back to the 13th century. John Rogers then came along and constructed the very beautiful re-work and frame which was a masterpiece in itself. The book was found in the garbage during the early 1970's by my stepfather, who in turn gave it to me. The book is said to be around one hundred and fifty years old. As I looked for the right picture to let you know how I'm feeling inside, I believe this is one of those rare combinations of a painter's and a writer's gift, for mankind to share.

It is my hope you might see and feel what I've been feelin', since I've come to know the spiritual side, which weighs heavier and is more powerful when a simple heart-felt picture shows clearly, "love's the reason why."

On the other hand, the words tell a story of needed salvation for the sinful man who cares only for himself, stemming from the things of worldly tradition; and we all know too well, how bad habits are hard to break!

Realize, the spilling of innocent blood poured out unto death by the Holy Lamb of God, will not go unavenged by our Father in heaven.

Paul Eugene Barr

Pauly Barr

Introduction

People dream of power, ruling their own country or countries one day, even the entire world as it will come to pass. However, there is this constant conflict of interest in which every country figures its way is better, while trying to downgrade the hardships of poverty and human injustice labeled tradition, mainly because of prejudice and favoritism. They tell you only what they want you to hear, hoping you'll believe and do nothing while they continue their onslaught, suppressing you to work for them with little or no regard until you are no longer needed. If you're lucky enough to retire, your employer may give you a cheap gold watch or a pat on the back as you're walking out the door. After a few years into retirement and being happy, finally able to do some of those things you always dreamed about when you were working. Unexpectedly a notice comes from your old company concerning a quarter reduction in your pension plan. You're standing there, numb, thinking I can't believe what I'm reading. Is this the real American dream, from the proud and happy to the poor and depressed? In essence it's more like the all-American nightmare! Freedom means many things especially those chosen who have been, (after a while) exempt for the duration, like people of the arts. Those who excel are, writers, painters, musicians, athletes, actors and even special trades people that were given spiritual talents, avoiding the plight of suffering at the lowest level of life, excluding the third-world situation. There's a third-world situation in many of our own states throughout America, and when will that ever get addressed; like down south in Mississippi for example, not to mention many other countries as well. Because we don't live there, we can't see the sorrowful conditions. It's just too unreal but it is true!

I'm not so happy that you have had to taste much of this wasteland but you have not had to eat and swallow it, like the poor. In order to do the Lord's work the burden weighs heavier at times on those who do His will, than those who do not. If you stay on the path, your reward will be waiting when this unlawful system comes to its abrupt end. Those who have suffered in so many sad ways, "in that, who could tell you of it, or how to let it out from within when you can't. Feeling life take everything away when you've reached out for an answer, replacing it with nothing that only you could know, keeping it to yourself until what little bit left, is gone." If it were not for good people like yourselves, or my friends I've found along the way while doing what I came here to do, (I've known many times inside) I wouldn't have made it without you. I love all of you to the max and will forever. Maybe I can repay you in some small way for someone you love that might need help, when it's on the line and there's nothing anyone can do as a person except keep faith through being hopeful, doing what's right. If things work out we can hold the missing joy together once we get our friends back on course. I have only this book of lyrics an poetry to offer in belief of yesterday's death and resurrection of God's only begotten Son, Jesus Christ at Calvary. I've heard countless times people say there is no God or there is but one God and no Son, so I'll just pray to God and skip everything else, just in case there is something out there that can hear me. Though I say unto you, focus on what you've been taught. "How could this Omnipotent Almighty Creator of life dwell in everything everywhere and share not with anyone that He could trust, that is of Himself?"

Think about it. Come on people! It's up to you to seek and believe as it will come to pass like yesterday did, though who has been able to see, and who really cares if it does or not. If you can't see it or you don't want to believe, maybe you're unsure or afraid to change because of what your friends might say, then what good is any of this to anybody who's searching for the real truth in God. Do what you've gotta do but tell me, how much effort does it take to say a three minute prayer, even if you don't believe in nothin'? It can't hurt. Before this is all over, those of you who don't give a damn, "you're gonna wish you did!"

We're already too far gone with drugs, alcohol and let's not forget true love, seems to crush even the strongest of hearts at one time or another, when we seek our own desires instead of letting God show us the real way, "but who's got time for that, right?" I've heard the young people say if it feels good do it, because it's right and how could God make anything so beautiful for it to be deceitful or wrong. When the children are young and feeling their way, you couldn't tell them as they know everything. Though I say unto you, one who develops a love for sweets and food ends up fat, hardly ever losing the unsightly weight. Or the one who loves to drink until his liver and blood is like that of which he has drunk, finally dying from some form of alcoholism. How about the one who swears to you while he's choking his brains out, "I love smoking and chewing tobacco." I can quit anytime, but later the poison called nicotine turns his breath bad, rotting his gums and teeth, turning the cells into lung cancer or an emphysema case. In reality they have all become addicted and don't have the guts or will power any more to fight back, though you must fight back against the evil force and be a winner! Realize the dark side wants you to do his bidding, but don't give in, seek the light through Christ. He will help ya win. So take another hard look my friend. Everything the worldly people call right doesn't always mean it is, as you will find out when the infectious disease of iniquity passes by your door!

When I was young there was a brother who spoke saying, "I have been to the mountain top and I have seen." He saw that someday all mankind will be free in peaceful harmony with the living, loving God. I was taken to a secret place when I had lost my spirit. Where I was taken became the lightest shade of emerald green throughout the inside area which seemed like a rock formation all around me. The oval green, yellow and red seal of God kept me there suspended for a few seconds, then returned me my life. Believe what you will but please take some time away from your busy life, rest and search in a peaceful manner from what you do for a living. Try a little more to learn the blessed way for your children's sake, if not your own. Those of you who already know God's will, will hopefully find my work a joy to read often and come to understand. Those who feel that the end coming means total destruction of you and the ones you love, and the world. I can tell you without any doubt, hold no fear for tomorrow's day if you have accepted Jesus as your Lord an Savior. When the hour comes like a flash of lightening it will strike! God and Jesus will then take what goodness is left in this world, bringing you away unto Them, "safe from any more suffering." The wrath of God will then be poured out upon the evil dwelling within His creation. It will be called the battle of Armageddon. The false prophet who's already entered the world near the Middle East will try "spinning you a different tail, but don't believe what you see!" He will deceive many because you won't take the time to "heartfully pray" that God would reveal one of the wolves in sheep's clothing to you. This is what is meant in the Bible when it says, "the devil can come as an angel of light." Only Jehovah God holds the true power of the light. I ask you to reach inside and hold on somehow in faith for a few more years, because the time is almost upon us to see who holds the true spiritual power of good verses evil. Those people who are Antichrist and don't want to believe, will see the truth being dealt to you at a costly price.

Let me share with you that it grieves my heart something awful, knowing there are many Christian people who seem to forget rather quickly when they were filthy wretches, saved only by the grace of God. They become holy rollers with their holier-than-thou attitudes, stumbling everywhere they go with their blinders on condemning the unsaved, as well as ranking on the flock and other churches. It's easy to see today no one is going to agree one hundred percent about anything anyone has to say, or the things he or she may do; especially seeing the Christians can't even agree on what God has given us in terms of His Holy Word to believe in. How could any of us get across to another when just about everybody wants to be an unmoving separate entity within the body. Realize through prayer and fasting that 2000 years ago Jesus set the example and the mission is still one of repentance and salvation. And now wouldn't ya know it, yes sir-ree, today it's still repentance and salvation all the way through and after the millennium reign. Wherever you are, it will be there for all to see just as it was in the days of old. Let us step down from our pedestal, roll up our sleeves and go down into the valley where the sorrow is, leading by that same example; so the unsaved soul would hopefully see the spiritual truth receiving the same grace, and come to believe in Jesus. That's where it's all at people, it's that simple. The year of the deuce there-of, (before or there-after) will be the calling card of our Lord and free men again is our prayer and song to an Almighty God. May the Father and Son watch over you and your loved ones before the rapture comes.

(M)

Table of Contents

65. Abortion
    (neither side is the winner here)
66. Looking At You
67. Where Is This Love
68. Morality Will Live
    (within the children who seek it)
69. You Are His World
    (and we must repent and believe)
70. Sincere Talk
    (makes for a closer walk)
71. Being In
    (but not part of this world)
72. The Gay Side
    (it's nowhere)
73. Talk Freely To Me, I'm Listening
74. In The Year 3070
75. It Takes Two To Reach There
    (and it works both ways)
76. Jews For Jesus
77. There's Got To Be Another Way
    (for you and me)
78. I'm Searching For You
    (the prisoner)
79. Cremation
80. The Written Word
    (all of it)
81. Freedom's Reality
82. A Bluesman's Song
83. Memory
84. People Just Talk To Talk
    (and never do or say anything)
85. Is It Always Going To Be Goodbye
86. Magic Carpet
87. The Airplane Ride
88. Waiting For Truth
89. My Personal Flavor
90. Life's Second Chance
91. The Secrets We Carry
92. The Big Ladle
93. One Two Three
    (why is it we can't see)

An Afterword.

(R)

A Little Daily Ditty

"When you first rise
choosing your desired threads
to meet the day,
don't forget to greet your Lord Jesus
our Father God,
putting a song in your heart
and a smile on your face;
yeah, it's really okay   (smile)"

Our Father

The distance so great
within,
You being up there
an' me down here.

Needing one another very much
rides in us all,
as time flows throughout
our feelings
of why
the calm has taken
so long
never being freed,
until You stopped by
letting me look upon Thee.

While Your love shapes
the universe
one resting in the other,
making tomorrow
what it should have been
before,
asking to walk along with You
forever
from my heart to Yours.

We shall lay on our bed
of tides
seeking the motion only You
can give
with Your wishes in life
for eternity's day,
being brought
to us
in Your own time and way
- - -

You're My Every Thought

Mom and Dad
we want you to know
as a family,
you, like ourselves
have had our ups and downs,
but we're all here to share
and hold
that bond of love together,
you showed
through the years.

Wherever you are in flesh
or spirit,
the children finally understand
what you wanted
by working an' caring so much
pulling us through,
meant a lot by far.

"Because of you both
could we honestly and truthfully
grow,
we love you very deeply
maybe even more
than you will ever know"
- - -

The Way Out

The world's fortune will be conveyed
to the likes of horrified people tending this
inhumane game.

We have wined, dined, and gladly earned
those wrinkles
turned to a hardened day
taking it out upon our children's age,
"when the Creator tells of His ways
how we can pass back through the
cross
keeping the ugliness away."

Your traits of misfortune have cost beyond
the score
sealing off the passageway
putting us under your own downfall,
where love is merely honest discipline
you have loved your way to and from what?

Hurrying around with methods of
useless faults,
telling your children who's in their teens
wishing they were around twenty-five
thinking the world's really alive,
"money for material things is the ultimate drive."

When the children reach themselves
morally
it's a different story,
being cast away, without knowing any glory.

God is more than pleased to create
a spiritual worth within
some will learn,
living in a fortune already conveyed
before we were sent here
showing our people,   there is a better way
- - -

3

A Brother's Word

I, like the other brothers
want to share
helping the children find their answers
with a certain Book,
prophesying events unfolding now to the
new world,
which is only fair.

To know everything we wish
we did
though this pressure around us
involves things yet known,
and no man
has all the answers
where it comes and goes.

Only you in time will know
if there is prosperity in your future
and by what goal
should there be to seek.
Through faith in heart
you will find
His authority given truthfully.

"It makes no more to me
for you will do what you will,
maybe fall
as many have fallen,
however you will see it coming
and it will happen,"
so prepare making the changes within
before your world becomes
meaningless.

We're smoothing away the roughness
of where one walks
without feeling the pain
in every step
- - -

4

Faith To Freedom

We have to leave this scene
behind us
taking the children
and older people with us,
for we're needing them
just as much
as they're needing us, too.

Helping one another
rebuild
all over again
finding our place together
making sure before we go,
showing our young that's learning
from the older people
who all ready know
who loves us the most.

"Those sensitive dreams
once we held when just a child
understanding later
faith, kindness and spiritual belief was the
answer,
for it's the key from above
opening your door to freedom."

We have to leave this scene
behind us
taking the children
and older people with us,
for we're needing them
just as much
as they're needing us, too

- - -

Finding Some Time

Sitting in your seat
reflecting on what you saw,
how it looked
and made you feel, back then.

Never seeming to be
as you would see
with feelings in touch,
like a simple candle giving its
lighted glow
through the darkness,
to a fast moving stream
of fresh clean water splashing about
on a warm sunny day.

Quick like a heartbeat
faster than a ray
of light,
"your eyes catch a rare glimpse
of a beautiful sight
painted in your memory forever,
though it never seems to last
long enough,   to one"
- - -

We came here to play for you
and our mission is to ease
the hurt and pain
that you might feel relief enough
to see,
before you leave.

The world isn't fair because there's
a choice to be made
and it's up to you to make
the passing grade.

We're asking to crossover the barrier
which surrounds your heart
so love could reach through.
Praying with hope in trust
receiving a cure from the heartaches
you've been dealt
by your family or so-called friends.

We'll take you by the hand
crossover the storm together
showing your troubled heart
God's Word and plan,
never leading you astray.

We're no different than you
where you are is where we were,
reaching out in time
before the infection sweeps you away
never realizing until it does,
what it's gonna feel like crossing over
the separation

(con't)

7

being locked away spiritually.

Hearing many people call out for help
down the road
to the One who holds the only
key
were answered immediately
by Christ and Jehovah God
who set 'em all free!

This isn't a fairy tale people
and we're not trying to run your life,
we're here showing you the
deepest insight.
Now that you've listened to our message
given by the cornerstone of life
to share
are you willing to become a little more
aware?

Are you willing to crossover
with thoughts in heart
accepting this Lord Jesus
slain for you,   then resurrected
on the third day?

If His world is truth
like I'm hope'n you're think'n,
what will He do for me
if I open the door and let Him into
my heart,
could it really be I would know
and feel
a brand new start?

After I've been shown then given
the test
I want to become strong enough
making it through,
because there's no way I'd ever
walk away
once I knew this truth was real,
and stay like the rest

- - -

Love Them Burgers

Burgers and burgers
or cheeseburger deluxe
ooohh
they're so outa' sight,
I think of little else
when I'm munching away
keeping those hungries at bay
on any given day or night.
Yeah,
"totally awesome
and such a delight
cooking up warm   juicy,
you know
they're gonna taste
just right"
- - -

For Us To See

Given sight through light
for us to see
a moment encircled in aura,
witnessing yesterday's path.

Being used by others
we've learned what people do
for kicks these days,
"never searching out those ways to stay
in love,
just taking it for granted."

For you to see
how it was in my eyes
for me to see
how it would be behind yours,
willing to unite
into one
hoping our feelings never become
undone.

Honor must be upheld
to realize God's spiritual love
within one another,
"while others tell of
their way
only to fall from grace
but no, not you."

All these feelngs for our love
I want us to give
that life might show
a better way,
granting the purity
of what we really mean
to each other
through our excited hearts,   forever
- - -

He Will Always Ride Free

A free ridin' man
when he held his cycle
within his hands.
Leanin' back
getting on the road
making it the only way
there was to do,
the brothers that rode with him
I know they all knew.

A brother to all he met,
then later
hearing of the two abreast
riding back alone
holding onto each other.
His hair blowing free
like the windy breath he felt
inside his chest,
listening to the sounds
of his bike's chores
cruisin' at your side
trying to put an end to those
unlawful laws of confinement,
they hang
over your ears and eyes.

The proud biker
knows what his scooter can do
because we know he knew then
how it had to be
and how it's been,
setting the people free
with his purple-colored Harley.
Together with him
you see his beauty in realism
we will grow to know,
he will always ride free
just Pappy and me
- - -

The Realization

I've realized there's more to life
than you or me,
we've got to connect in spirit
if we want to be free.
I've tried to reach where you are
you've had to sense it coming from a far.

You know how the world is today
so different than yesterday,
"with changes needed morally
to survive,
teaching our children in truth
is better than showing them how to
live a lie."

The road gets greater and greater
as we climb
the enemy doesn't want us to find
the answer,
"like why won't the beginning
be the forever it really is,
is what we're all searching for."
I guess we understand at some point in life
the value
of everyone's feelings that touch us,
by not throwing them away.

Given love through grace we learn
forgetting no one who is real,
placing our pain into a depth
where there will be no more phony barriers
upsetting our truth,
"for the people you've tried to help
through the years
will find their way home because of you,"
(realizing one for another
is the only way
we're going to make it happen)
- - -

You Are Life's Worth
(what's left of it)

We were born into darkness
of a world
many people can't see
and most of us will stay this way,
unless love for Almighty God, Jesus Christ
and the Holy Spirit
who are always near,
becomes the one true reality
in this invisible spiritual bondage
we face,
since the first children looked away
from our Father.

Sending His Son
to us
many years ago,
God will do so again
when time itself
is nowhere to be found.

Days pass into years
yet the hour cometh to see
freedoms gain
within your heart and soul,
it dwells forever.

Peace be with you if you can
find it,
"for many talk
though very few really know
what it takes
to live and find such a purpose,
as it slips through
your hands
like sand in an hour glass"
- - -

Her For Him And Him For Her
(as it was once)

Our world we find
is more than just one,
for man and woman enter themselves
seeing a world exists through their own being
as well as what's given them
by way of birth here.
This world,
unless you have been granted a part
seems unsteady indeed.

The time is consumed
as everything turns about mostly for a loss
because people use one another
instead of making those changes
holding their bond together,
(figuring it doesn't matter
there's so many to choose from)

We look to someone or something
to bring back the way it was
when you both knew
you were made for one another,
and nothing could ever change
the hidden meaning of why you yourself
let go.

When attention and affection disappear
becoming less than a separation noticed
made from the same pattern like before,
carrying it with you and refusing not to change
is where the problem lies.

"Realize if you only would, loves hope for you both,
in what's still there before it's too late
when you first reached out and
touched
each other's feelings"
- - -

The Street People

Tethers of threads
hang from these old used cloths
and shoes,
it's the best I wear.
Caring less about status
many laugh off to the side
when I pass by.

"Where do you think they're going
I ask myself,
nowhere fast either
I'm afraid."
Face it people, it isn't you out here
having to live like this.
Don't say there isn't
another way
you know it's you, not me
that's fallen prey.

Though you can't see
it's all I'm ever going to need
in this trip,
"because no one's gonna help me
find me,
is why the street's my home
until we're dead and gone.
That's right people
until we're all dead,   and gone.

Guess that's how you want it to be
cause that's how it is,
thinkin' to myself
out here in the bitter cold weather,
if I lay my head down and get some rest
will I be alive
when the morning comes
is my hope,   and ultimate test"
- - -

14

Take This, It's Yours

Power, majesty, and light
will redeem us from the night
if we seek it through our heart and soul,
or never find control.
To reach you, to teach you
keeping you by the Lord's side,
He's not going to let nothin' bad happen
to ya   no!
He's not going to let you get taken
for a ride.

Give yourself a fighting chance
"know in your searching heart
this is the way you can confide,
yes,   you truly can confide."
Never again will you suffer being
denied
because nobody cares or has the time
to show us what's morally right
without losing sight.

Open your heart line,
it's not always bad things after bad
this is not how the Lord works.
We've been led to living in the monster's lies
so only a few can survive,
you've got to trust me
seeing ahead
love's the reason why
keeping you by the Lord's side.

He's not going to let nothin' bad happen
to ya   no!
He's not going to let you get taken
for a ride.
"Know in your searching heart
this is the way you can confide,
yes,   you truly can confide"
- - -

Why The Rain

When gentle droppings of rain
fall to the earth's floor
sometimes in puddles
sometimes on you,
I find myself
listening so closely
the sounds turning into echoes
falling differently
to a pattern of placement.

It's like a dream you always
dreamt
that brings your feelings to realize,
we must pursue our dreams
regardless of what's in our way
when it's right.

Tears like rain
have washed my face
flooded my thoughts
shaken by visions,
the spiritual food we need
will be thrown away
by some of the children today.

As I try not to think why
the echoes heighten
and I hear the rain again,
while my thought realm
can't hold back the bottled up
sensitivity
of their tiny little feelings
they keep to themselves,
until it's too late.

Don't do it
don't choose to go away

(con't)

from me,
we need you!
It's cuttin' me up inside
bringing my feelings to nothin'
trying to reach you!

"Look,
don't put this trip on me alone
you've got to pray it through
the measure has been given to all of you!
If I walk away,   empty
without you
our dreams will just be broken dreams."

For me
there's only the rain
tears and you,
were all that's left that's real
in truth
can't you see it,   feel it?

Christ dripped His blood out
for you
then died of a broken heart
on the cross.

Come on now people
get real
you've got to take it in and receive
believing life through faith
is the dream of all dreams,
becoming one   within the Son
- - -

I Defend Rock'n Roll
(Blues and Christian too)

We have kept these words
tucked away in our hearts
until the dust
that collects on them
finds you.
A note
for a note
a tune
for a tune
has taken us this far.

By throwing away the little good
we've found
brings tears I've cried
to loosen the world's evil grip
on me,
"of meaningful hope in truth
given of grace
you may know to see,
and we have."

We must forgive the confused
they can't see through
the invisible grayish lining that
covers all
living and dead,
like the promise I made
within my heart
believing in the ones with gifted insight,
was the only way in return
reaching those chosen few in spirit.

I defend rock'n roll
and I'm not gonna be so blind
like many critics who say they know
the truth,

(con't)

when they don't even know anything
about music,
or what God's doing at all.

To hold
this special goodness
our brothers an' sisters have given
it's what I'm gonna do,
"by safeguarding
the only note
and tunes
bringing the sound we love
like no other
that's brought us this far,
will take us
the rest of the way home"
- - -

One Hand Washes The Other
(so I've been told)

Now everybody knows
the ones
who have made it to the top
in whatever it was
that got them there.
You've had your say many times
and done
what you've wanted to do.

You have seen your day
come and go
even though the world needed,
you came through.
We've known many a good man
through the billions of souls
upon this earth,
yet there was no answer
like you.

You needed life and
gave,
people in turn
made you what you are.
"While you're free
to do as you please
the poor men and women carry their
empty dreams
to slave for the few pennies and
security
they will never see until later,
when the spiritual change comes."

Do what you can
devise a plan
reach out your hand,
give back to them

(con't)

18

a piece of their broken
homeland.
Why do you think so many have walked
before you
finding a way to make it,
but never lifted a finger
to see anyone else pull through
except themselves!

- - -

The Veterans Of War
(goin' back to their world)

Greed
for land, wealth and power
though the ol' cliche is
stopping the spread of communism
shoved you brothers off to war,
keeping you there
until your time in country was over.

"Trained like an animal for survival
kill or be killed,
many brothers in every branch
never making it back
messed up your head,
while getting out alive
was your only real worry."

Once home
all we wanted was our freedom
an' end to the red tape
in receiving our deserved benefits
which the damned warmongers and profiteers
keep delaying or taking away,
(being able to go someplace we felt was
home
starting over,
though many never did find home
like it was
before we left)

The veteran dreams
pieces of their bloody nightmares
in firefights,
wanting to forget
the incoming rounds, exploding bombs, gassings,
causing torn, burning heartaches
forcing his spirit to awaken

(con't)

19

in a cold feverish sweat!,
during the early morning hours.

It's not the little people in
America
or any other country,
but those who rule over us
refueling our life's long grief.

No matter what democracy
we're under,
we all fight for truth
freedom,
our families and friends
standing as one in our belief,
"whatever life was lost
limb or limbs,
you will be given back
in the end,
especially our POW'S and MIA'S"
- - -

Stop Spreading His Lie
(it's too much like bread and butter)

When you figure you know,
then let me know
how you plan on leaving
this place.
People have been saying
one to another
his death was of natural causes
or it looked like a suicide,
when you've known all along
who's been killing who and why,
still you try and hide
in the lies of a liar's eye!

You're well off
but you give very little up
to those who need,
so you think
the flight is right and for you
real,
but your profession you stole
your life is wasted
when you borrow, you steal!

"You'll watch your own brother
rot and bind up inside
because you bought out your
soul,
now your wrong is right to you
spreading those lies, lies, lies
until you die!"

It's hard for the good people
fairly young in the world
to understand these changes
that come so quickly,
"but I know the ones

(con't)

20

who will try and make do,
for they're the ones that want to be
like you."

Knowing the evil way is
not ours
you will see the difference through time,
so tell Christ and God
the truth
tell 'em you need 'em
tell 'em you love 'em,
and before I see Them
I'll do the same too

- - -

The Trials Of Growing Up

At times the burden seems more
than one can carry
especially when you're young
not knowing which way to turn,
I can understand
where it would be a little scary.

Realize it's only a trial
that everyone goes through
and yes,
I know, I know
it seems like an uphill heavy-duty task
but your problems will pass.

He's not going to give you more
than you can deal with,
though you must build on faith
finding someone to talk to
you can trust
if you're not ready to look into
the Word just yet.

Your life means something special
so don't move slow
because sooner or later
you've got to show.

"Before you decide and after
you do
think about the Being above
that's so strong,
He's not going to steer you wrong."

His names are many
with one written
on His thigh,
you can call from any place, anytime

(con't)

you don't even need any money
and that's no lie.

If you succeed in finding the path
it's not going to be an easy trade-off
yet your sorrow will lessen
making you feel
revived,
"checking things out in a whole new
faith
pushing those crummy demons far away
and outa' your face,
your tender spirit will grow
to survive"

- - -

Friendship's Road

Friendship means
always be there truthfully
for one another.
Try understanding each side
of things
before doing anything crazy.

(Let our respect and love
for life
surge through us forever)

When one thought needs another
your heart will fire up
the flame
if it's real,
"that we may never
have to feel sorry later
when we both take the time
in giving,
through thick an' thin"
- - -

Blind
(I didn't believe I could be, but I was)

Being blind
is more than one way
I could ever know,
though my eyes can see
I too am blind in many ways.
Never seeing the ugliness
in this world
for those who are,
was in your favor.

The pain it caused
has taken your colors,
but only for a while longer.
What can be done
wishing like other children
we could go out some where and
have fun?

I have no power
to help anyone see, hear
speak
or relate to this emptiness
inside our being.
"I believe there were reasons
for our problems,
some are given,   many we cause."

Sight or no sight
the One who has made you and I
will heal our inner soul
delivering us,
opening the closed door
finally walking through,
doing all those neat things
the other children and grown-ups do

- - -

The Children's Love To You

There's no sound
more innocent,
laughter
so precious,
their touch
warm and soft
than that of a child,
if but a moment
- - -

A Child's Blessing

One's self-centeredness
brings no vision of joy
upon his or her soul,
for giving His real love to us
shows the artificial warmth in their own heart
of choice.

While being around those types of people
you knew they never really learned or cared
like you or me.
"After the beginning of man
time has burdened us
with bitterness,
though it has to be understood
the curse must be lifted
as it was given."

We did not love enough
trusting our Father
who is trying to teach us
the life He is of
and the other part called sin,
who's plotting to control
then destroy the temple of goodness
within you
as it well seems.

"It was a dream
of a dreamer's dreams
one could imagine
finding the colored array of life's offering
again
for this generation."
The children sing and praise, hoping
God will turn the tide
so we no longer feel inside
we've got to hide away
until He brings us home to stay
- - -

Mabel
(they'll find out)

Still fussing with those few skimpy
decorations
around the window,
changing them with every mood.
I wonder how far away
her family lives,
for I heard someone say
it was only a short drive to here
though no one will stop by
and care.

After they had Mabel conveniently
put away
her worldly goods taken,
you know it was planned that way.

"Sad and helpless
she tries to regain her thoughts,
gasping, reaching to communicate
with someone
who will piece her words together
giving back her sense of
direction an' dignity."

Soon she forgets another day is before
wasting into yesterday
the answer kept in secret
when someone does visit,
until the time to make for somewhere
draws near.

Your turn carrying moments
you will wish
never having pulled on your own family
when the hours are long in coming,
feeling alone, unwanted, unloved
inside your little room!
- - -

Where Skies Stay Blue

From sunrise to sunset
looking into sky blue spaces
brightly filtered yellow rays
glistening through patterns in
cotton-like candy clouds floating by,
centering around wherever your view
with a magnitude of warmth.

(For those people who can only feel
or sense such a time,
to the ones who are told somehow
when there was no way possible
for them to know
a day
has shown itself,
with crystal clear beauty)

Your eyes surrounding themselves
with water
hoping to recapture this
peaceful rest,
though words nor pictures
will ever express this sensation
I've found,
where skies stay blue
- - -

Guide The Children Safely Home

Many times
we have seen
the gifted, the strong
the weak
even the slick
find their way in this world,
but never the unknowing.
They have no answer
to where or why they are
or what they do
so differently than you.

"Being unsure
taking advantage comes easy,
though who can really see
one's true side
in the short time you're with them."

My only hope is
you will guide the children
safely through
wherever they're headed,
that we may finally learn
what's locked away within their hearts
and yours,
while we try again
to keep them
from getting abused
- - -

No Title - No Label

Sometimes the way you feel
inside
can't be said in words
when you want to hear them
spoken,
right then by someone.

Somehow you're sure you know
though the person you're near
may not come forth
afraid of saying the wrong thing,
"while searching for those emotions
that keep from us
the why's and ways of it all."

(If only I could see
for sure to say
I know I'd try for you,
if I knew of
what makes you listen,
and care)

When the time arrives to hear
what gives,
words taken in by you
with hope
finding our true feelings
for each other,
leaving you an' me with something positive
to work on.

Through timeless heart-felt memories
we learn to hold the warm rays
of sunlight and rainbows,
"bringing us around as one
if it's meant to be,
cleansing life's tide within
that you might know, I love you"
- - -

A Smile
(you can make happen)

Can you still see their smiles
from before
and now,
"so pretty and real
letting you know
the sensitive creation
of all those many precious moments
they have put into your weight
of being,
and you their's."

All this joy for you
brings the aura's glow
around your soul
so full in worth
never being equalled with anything,
outside of your karma.

Making the heart warmer and
closer
for our life's willingness
will shine
no matter where we walk
along this path,
"bringing us to see
their smile reach with laughter
from the inside of you"
- - -

For You

Because you are somebody special:
I'm writing to let you know
when you have the time to spend,
the many years of toil
have taken their toll
from your heart,   (mine too)

I wish I could have helped somehow
when you were hurtin',
but there wasn't anything I could do
to keep away the pain
that reached you
or the people you loved in this world
while we were together.

If there was any other way to avoid
the sorrow
I wish it could have been that way
for you.
I wish I could reach inside
and take out what's been hurting ya
so much,
yet how can I when I know many things were
destined to be!
While it torments my soul
realizing, it's something I never wanted to believe,
though we can release the pain
and feel free.

"Everything you've ever seen or felt
about life
flows inside with purpose,   thinking;
happiness above all suffering
is for real happiness once we reach there,
making it a little easier
going back to you
seeing our families live again,
like we used to do"
- - -

Everyone's Dream

Everyone dreams measurably
from youth
finding love
one beautiful day.

When the search is hopefully completed,
something goes wrong
they try again
until you hear them say,
I've fallen in love
for sure.

"I wish I could be
next to you
touching, holding and
feeling numb all over,
taking a deep breath
melting away into the universe
finding a righteous place
where you get to keep what you
feel first."

Me,
I just want to be inside love
never to fall,
devoted one to another
giving our all
- - -

Your Beliefs And Mine

You are what you are
and you believe
what you will.
I am
what I am
and I believe what
I believe,
for this is my belief.

"It's either evil
or you
there's nothing anyone
can do,
as the chosen have found out
where life's been keeping us
within its course."
While awareness is generally tossed
something we know an' feel inside
just has to be fair
and should not be lost.

Noticing inner findings to believe,
He has told me nothing
but you,
"you He has told everything
bringing us away from these enduring ways
if your belief
is within the written Word
of the spirit,
it will be done."

Carrying your sights ahead
ending those strains of constant
disbelief
when things go right,
or your belief to a point
doubting
when things go wrong, for the moment
- - -

33

Life's Blues

No,
I don't know about you
where you're from
why you're here
tearing up my world,
wish I did.
People realize,
things look bad and we're hurtin',
(seems like we've all been hurting
for each other
a long time coming)

We can sense this trip
isn't taking us anywhere
fast
and we're tired of waiting, pretending
to be a family
we haven't been in generations.

You so-called human beings
in power
stealing the love
from our children's dreams
replacing it with ambitions for
yourselves,
shoving neglect and poverty
on us
until it's too late!

"I feel their hearts crying in the night
for you, themselves,
saying, make straight the way
but you won't listen!
Those dark evil desires can't defeat
our love
in light of the living Word,
demanding compensation for the

(con't)

many tears
I see fall from the children's cheeks,
is long overdue!"

No,
I don't know about you
where you're from
why you're here
tearing up my world,
wish I did.
You can't feel our sorrow
because of what you've been doin'
all these years,
the children have no tomorrow.

You know
I'm standing in your way
with the ability to see the truth.
You say
it's either you or me
but somebody's comin' down hard,
and He's gonna take you out
at a heavy cost,   to you.

"And when it's happening
I'm not going to feel a thing
for ya,
so chew on that for awhile and tell me
how you like it!"
Your evil power
wealth or literary degrees
will not take you sinners anywhere,
but hell!
- - -

Reaching The Past
(is tomorrow's answer)

My spirit cries out
and says to me,
there's only one hope in likeness
of this world today.
"So humbleness
yes,
where are you
my friend?"
- - -

Look But Don't Laugh
(because it could be you later on)

You must be aware
when you see people
talking aloud with a muttering slur
while standing or walking along,
though there isn't anyone there
talking back to them,
yet you can't help but stare.

"What makes them that way
will it happen to me?
It's the pressure
from below the world
that holds no grace
of how you look or what you say."

The sight isn't pretty
and if you catch yourself
doing these things,
avoid it by using your heart and
mind together.

Close your lips gingerly
fighting it off
up in your head
using inner strength,
keeping the ugliness away
that wills its presence
on you
or one you may know
- - -

Understanding

Looking out and in for someone
like you
while traveling through time,
wondering if you would be hoping
to share this heart of mine.

"Within our hearts beating so fast
I'm feeling these feelings
for you
or because of you I can't deny.
Is your heart telling mine
this means something to you as well?
A gifted woman there's no doubt
knowing of thy beauty,   love
you would never go and sell."

Maybe we're where we are
for now
to know our longing
until I see you before me some day
some crazy kinda way,
understanding how it should be
being brought together
forever.
Creation's love will find us passing from
flesh to spirit
the hour knowing the time.

As I dream about looking into your eyes
they feel close
like the heavenly skies,
where the beauty of it all
has no reason to lie.
In wanting to stay together
makes us a little more free
through this awesome gift of life,
I hope
you will always see,   to be with me
- - -

Don't Leave Me Alone

Is there something wrong this distance
I sense,
seems out of reach
one from another
as we work side by side
in all our different ways,
from day to day.

Fighting this emptiness
of being alone,
"you know it's not what you want
to feel.
It takes away the happiness
we gain
replacing it with a throbbing pain."

It doesn't have to be this way
an' you can help me if you try,
reaching into the spiritual side
discovering the ancient lie.

If you could see
to notice
helping make the change in mood
getting through,
a fulfillment will show the beauty
of how close we all can be.

"Meaningful heart
we must learn to give
every day, every way together
no matter what you do by yourself
or a group,
while we defeat this bad feeling
that tries bringing us down,
because nobody should be left alone.
You can turn it around
into something very special, like you."

- - -

Let's Journey Together

It's all right now my new-born
friend
we traveled this path before
and will do so again,
for the truth you hold
makes me want to give
and begin to live.

"Your warmth and light
can take away this dark loneliness
from me,
where there is no more."

To ponder
searching for ourselves
inside dreams
wandering carefully through,
sights unforeseen.

Don't hinder any of my friends
in joining together
that's what we want to do,
working on life's real meaning
which many people call a trend.

"Wiser now
we're sharing His holy name,
the unexpected will
dawn
and love shall reign."

Soon
gathering on high together,
safe
without a lost trace
nearing the heaven's edge,
freed from the ugliest part
of our journey's dredge

- - -

His Creation

Where the church is
you can hear the bell ring out
its lovely sounds,
as I notice the small of the flock
enter
in the name of the Lord.

I believe they have tried
to confess their wrong,
though leaving unsown sorrow
returning to those sinful deeds
is all I've sensed
gripping them and me.

The Lord will be among us again
though many try taking His place now,
(yet humbleness is far away
from one who would deceive the sheep
before the Son and God)

Heaven rests above
our earth,
the church being apart
waits in unsheltered disarray
for the spiritual answer.

Visions flowing from multitudes
in color
like the purple-spaded flower
to the green an' red meadow of yellow buttercups
inside His arm,
"letting us know
we will be where we find ourselves
prevailing in thoughts to Him,
in what the world means to you
is what creation means
to Him,
through the life we lead"
- - -

Thank You

To those doctors, nurses,
therapists
and those involved in rescue,
"helping during a crisis
preventing the spread of a
serious disaster
or severely injured to recovery,
even if it meant giving up
your own life."

Saving precious lives
young and old alike
are able
to push away
any further suffering
that devours the soul within them
and you,
if you fail to do your best.

"You're very special people
doing what you can
always conscious of the
fine line,
while giving many comfort
in their time of need."

I hope this will see you through
my friend
as the patients you've mended
and people saved,
have made it clear; mention;
I'm sure
of your trust
and gentle worthiness
they'll cherish forever an' ever,
because you gave
- - -

Ascension Island Rainbow
(the symbol of man's fate for tomorrow)

Traveling in a rainstorm
headed down the mountain trail
rounding another corner
leaving behind the mountain side
sunshine broke out everywhere,
while the dampness and storm
faded away.

In the middle of all this confusion
a brilliant anchored rainbow
showing both ends inside the rock walls,
colors of red, yellow, green and purple
gleaming steadfast in the sunshine
seven hundred feet off the roadside.
Our van loaded with people kept on
cruising along
while nobody got excited or had much
to say,
guess to them it was just another day.

I know
they were caught up in thought
wondering why
at such an unexpected beautiful sight,
which was no ordinary rainbow by far.
Though in their hearts
I hope they rejoiced
to see the symbol of man's fate,
knowing a dream
was answered close and true
before some of the crew
- - -

Will You Remember
(God poured out His spirit into you)

The feeling has left
your being now
and will not like before,
come again.
Those few short years of time
we as children
have been answered with truth
that no man or demon can produce on this earth,
seeing the beginning of many signs
to come.

Many wondered in amazement
as to its whereabouts,
many already knew the secret
many cared less
and lied when asked of its nature.
You can slam your would-be door
you can program your computers
until they read your no answer.
You can play or listen to your favorite tunes
still the feeling will not come
to any of you.

Maybe you will try deceiving
the children for a while
but not for long,
who are younger now and were never told
of the spiritual feeling within them
that nobody wants to talk about.
The little joy of love
was given
"to awaken the world
that the older children will remember
in the future,
there is another way for them
and the ones
they say, they love"
- - -

43

Dreams Are Forever

Is there a prince or princess
here,
all those dreams
I kept so near
finding out at times
nothing's really clear.

"As our cycle meets the change
we refuse to accept with
pretending vein
costing our morality to lose it's range."

It's hard enough
staying where you are
though that's where you should be,
building on what you know
is you so true.

Dreams like the sun will never
turn cold,
our prince and princess
shall beat the hidden scheme,
forever living
in those priceless dreams
that can be kept
so dear
- - -

The Universe Of Enchantment

Day or night when you're
out there
where you want to be,
the world is yours
above and below.
During daylight
in keeping the sun's warmth
to twilight setting,
your spirit climbs upward
"as glistening stars
fill your wondrous sight
guiding with safe speed
flying closer,
reaching and grasping onto
stepping from one star to another."

Looking below
at the vast endless
world of moving beauty
stemming forever everywhere,
as the moon's lighted aura rings
are caught dancing
between the masses of sighted stars
while piercing colors
rush right through your soul;
making you feel and sense
a belonging
a love
in our dream of creation,
waiting for only you
to behold
- - -

I Love You

How much did You suffer
in the beginning
before time was,
only You know, Father.
It must have been great
for You to allow
all these years of plagues
and sorrowful events,
though there was some good
in all.

We are for real,
and it makes me so pleased
that my head
is really high for once
when I can be permitted
to think of You,
knowing now, You always were
and You always will be
loving me.
For You have taught
both
the good and bad children,
the meanings of

life,
     respect,
          love,
               discipline,
                    freedom,

          me
          - - -

The Coal Miner

The coal miner
had no other way to survive
from his hard-dug tunnels
when it was one of few choices
putting food on the table.

It's sad enough
the hell and suffering
you face the same problems
with many other trades.

"Your long existing miles
of worked mines
show the horrid black pain
inside your lungs."

While working below those depths
it takes a lot of heart
not knowing if you will make it
back up
smelling the same polluted air,
outrageous prices
in food and rent
that used to be worth working for.

From the cave in
brothers trapped inside
some dead, some alive
knowing possibly there is no way
the ones you love
if an' when they're dug free,
will see you
on the other side.

You're on top crying
clawing away, bleeding, praying,
trying to remove fallen dirt and rocks,

(con't)

"hoping on the way up
yours and theirs will be all right;
from chains, picks and shovels
to numbered machines and men,
you know the companies keep on
rigging it
so you're never gonna win!"

Being solemn
is a very precious thing
and it won't be much longer
until the coal miner
breathes life
for his family and friends,
knowing the reason
is for warmth
putting coal inside your bins
- - -

Divided

Divisions stemming
from our own fold
divide the millions of people
covering this house.
Divided we are in speech
divided we are in ever-changing cultures
divided we are by seas,
divided we are in high tech nuclear an'
chemical weapon usage.
"Divided we are by corrupt systems
of big business and
man's law,
leaving our house desolate."

Divided we are in greeds
which travel far from the ego, pride,
the dollar
relations of man, woman
moral values,
spiritual and material life masses.
Divided we are in science
according to right and wrong
experiments dealing with your life,
for man will never create anything
but more problems.

Divided we are in will,
being equal one to another
because man the child refuses his
fellow brother,
so heaven and hell exist.
"Division is our enemy bringing us down
to stay
when there's a better way,
but we do nothing
while struggling separately,
sadly lost in those

(con't)

cumbersome social levels."

Divided you will always
be
until your work is good work,
for Jesus needs no eyes
knowing the heart
to repair
because He is the
cornerstone;
many builders rejected
and will pay dearly
when Jehovah calls the purple trump
from within His left hand!
- - -

The Children Are Lost
(and need true direction)

These hurt twisted feelings
must go away
and grow anew,
as we all end up hurt by
someone
who forms a habit or likeness
of one.

"Sometimes when hurting someone
many times never knowing
you did,
while again
many times knowingly
you do!"

We all have been hurt so
we don't realize how much
we hurt others
when we're with them,
for it seems hard knowing
anymore
when we do or don't.

"Only when you discover
does the pain stay inside
needing precious time
no one knows of
to heal,"
formed from this world's
last days
of desperation is why,
likely more than not
we may never see,
though I am hoping for you to.

These hurt twisted feelings

(con't)

shall fade away
growing onward once again,
"if people would humble themselves
remembering how to ask
reaching out with the tiniest seed
of faith in hope
we could learn
what's wrong and right,
instead of getting lost through
sin
the true direction will begin"

\- - -

The Broken Piece

If you know what we are inside
that makes your children real,
when will you come back and
help us heal?
I realize it's not easy
for people to say anything to you, Lord;
you've been through it all,
though the suffering is real down here
and many fall.
What else can we do while we work
to get through
from here to you?

Trying to keep those problems away
in our own taught and given way,
"is why God held the world in darkness
those few hours
on that saddened day."

This isn't a toy anymore you play with;
we've all done enough tampering
with the broken piece
trying to find the Son's place, and yours.
Search out in truth, God's sworn enemy
who's destroying our youth
and put an end to the abuse.

"You have shredded its core
to shambles
now it means nothing more,
so don't tell me being torn in two
is something new to only you,
for I'm made of so many different pieces
right now
I've lost my shattered soul
and I don't know what to do!"
No, I, I just don't know what to do
while I wait here on you, Lord
- - -

Marriage's Honor

Of all the people
in this world
creation came your door.

When the moods change
like life itself,
try within
hold fast,
that you may find again
together,
rendering invincible
- - -

On A Scent

Life needed inside to acquire
the strength in our lives
is for the children
to build with,
so brother-man, don't throw your future
away
because you lack the heart
and guts
tracking life's scent of sorrow;
there was a beginning
you're here now,   there will be a spiritual end!

From one another searching our
inner depths
feeling an undeniable truth
letting out the pain through
relaxed talk,
if the direction held in realism
will hurt us no more,
we will find what were looking for.

"Love shall be first once again
and man will no longer
hang his own brother on a fixed
cross,
like they've done in those
dark days
trying to hide yesterday's corrupt past."
God searches the hearts of His
children
who are longing for answers
by resurrecting the destroyed truth.

"Although locked away and misinterpreted
are His words,
duties continue with the brothers
in giving back our share
of this rightful light"
- - -

The Book Of Life

I believe in Your words
You have given us,
though no one has been able
to step through this darkness
bringing them back to You Father,
as we have found ourselves awake somewhat
down here
but not too well I'm afraid.

"Your sheep have not been
properly fed
the world itself is almost dead,
while Your children turn out murders
or worse
by their own hand
through the evil one's design."
Your garden has been destroyed
as creation trembles
with distress,
waiting for the sacred cleansing hour.

I feel life in everything
dwindle,
having died here trying to find the
right page
the perfect stage
so we could have known
what You wanted us to do,
"through all those dreamless years
of us
loving ourselves
and not loving You, like we're supposed to;
returning a tiny portion of what
used to be
since the first word and breath was given
within You, Father,
to me"
- - -

Jesus Knows
(and so do you)

Oh why can't you see
it's being given unto you
and me,
oh why can't you read
read the signs?

It can never be your way
just for you
the brothers and sisters
that live next door or overseas,
they're apart of us to.

"The church, there is but
one
call it what you will
wherever you're from.

What good is it if only
a handful of people keep pulling
us through,
soon there will be nothing left
not even me or you!"

The temple rests within
yourself
which causes our families to disagree
produces more
of his dreaded disease.

You and I were made
to set all the children free,
but when I look into your eyes
and listen to your words
I cry inside,
because my heart tells me
you can't see
see the reasons why
- - -

Many Farmers' Seeds
(not being sown)

Holding valuable land
the seed grows our food
feeding at an endless rate
with rain and sunshine
with worked soil
that knows the farmer's touch,
"bringing sturdy crops of plenty
as you watch your fields
begin to produce another season
in hopes of giving back
one to another."

Life through life's resources
during those long days of preparation
for good honest consumption
without falsely treating these
vital foods,
before leaving the farm for market
is our hope.

"To the consumer's needs
resorting in pleas
facing hunger and beginning to see ahead
the need,
crying out saying
what's happened with our government
our store chains who fix the prices,
the farmer and his decaying deed."

Stop taking payoffs
and start planting a true seed
in feeding our people.
Though we may be poor
in many things,
basic food items should not be kept from
anyone,
especially the elderly!
- - -

Reasons For Reason

If you had to tell a lie
long as it wasn't against
the principles of truth,
these reasons
are honest enough,
for you have lied
because of the anguish that would not
cease and heal within another.

I know you would live your lie
so the poor souls would never have to
accept fate,
bringing them down even more
than one
should have to bear.

If a little fib or tale
will help you both see to stay away
from things
that make you lie wrongfully,
"you will always be without knowing
those uncertainties
waiting for the one
who does lie,   to deceive"
- - -

The Vision

I am a witness Father
in yesterday's death and resurrection of
Jesus Christ,
early one Easter morning
March, 1975.

As I lay asleep
a flood of bright white light came pouring in
between my eyes that awakened me.
I was watching the angels moving about
inside the light
numbering many,
when the two black squares-like boxes
appeared
neatly wrapped, then the third
being empty
opened and clear, except the seams
"representing the three days,"
(meaning the day God resurrected His only Son
from the grave)

My frightened state worsened when an evil voice
said to me,
"if you go, you will surely die!"
In my confusion of what to do
the vision of light left my sight
then returned
with a moment's flash
a couple seconds later,
leaving me with a path of markings
one day will see us through,
if you believe in my Lord Jesus
like I do,   too
- - -

Hoping To Share a Feeling

The things we must seek
are of life's ways
being created
on the Lord's green earth,
in search
of one's true touch
on our heart and soul,
which seems
to be a mystified dream
of this world today.

When will reality
be seen and felt by others
"who don't know what it is to care,
for giving means to share
loving you for what you are inside."

As our awareness deepens
within our minds
I find it harder
with the lessening of time,
this world taking us further away
one from another
until there is no more joy
to buy up
in this senseless hope
we have led amongst ourselves
for the many years,
because of unrepentant faults.

"Still the days pass us by
like none we've ever known
while the sorrow is like no other,
one does feel to cry
alone inside"
- - -

Gotta' Have Da Pizza

Pizza, pizza
that's my name
everywhere I go it's always
the same,
as I leave only to find myself
coming back,
though I try not eating too much
for fear of the big
fat attack.

It's true, people love me so much
because of my
scrumptiously delicious toppings
layered over a hot firm
crunchy crust,
which always carries a sweet
inviting aroma
that's brought me to fame.

Laughing and enjoying myself
with my friends
while woofin' down that ol' pizza
thinking,
it's the name of the game.

I've got a good funny feeling
if this keeps up
after the last little bite is gone,
I'm wondering
if it will be enough?

Ahh yes, munch munch
away
what can I say;
I really love da pizza   (smile)
- - -

Depths Of Height

Now that I've gone
on my way
leaving the things we have done
and will do again
when we can find the
right days.

"Being the guinea pig
as most of us are
made me burn within like a
red hot cinder,
I know
will never die out!"

I've found many a worthy
brother and sister
which brings me around
looking for you,
"because we are life's hope and gift
one to another
as I've seen and felt through our
Father,
who has shown you me
and me a few of you."

(Your faces
shine in my thoughts
like the beauty you mean
to me,
is why you are
for me,   to see)

Then before I can express my enchantment
of how I'm feelin',
you carefully slip away
leaving those depths of height,
all around me
- - -

No Honor Now
(but there will be tomorrow)

We have been led to
exist
in this life with little honor in ourselves.
Let me go my path
and don't label me
with your controlled guilt
of past doings,
dragging me with you into today
for your own evil trips
forced on others from birth
made uglier than filth itself,
an' we're not going to live like this anymore!

I've learned the difference between
right and wrong
that's my song
to those who are searching for truth,
which comes at a price
you've got to pay,
as I've walked my way through
the demonic side
of their projected spiritual nightmares.

When I leave this world
I'll fly with the light
of life,
knowing it's gonna make me feel
kinda nice
leaving behind the ugly strife
- - -

Poor Louise

Life's force is not yours
dealing with the future
of our children's true path,
obtaining your desires
from a frozen sperm bank
or using someone else's womb for money
is not the answer to this
grave mistake,
"forcing fate upon thousands of
orphan and foster children
who need a good home,
but you've turned your back on 'em!"

The women good or bad are blessed
for reasons
only One knows.
The ones that are blessed
want more
while the unblessed ones
bless themselves the
unloving way
conceived from the root of misdirection
named failure,
never admitting lost reason and feeling
for the divine creation of total love.

"The further away we choose
the further away from goodness
we will not, until later see in our
children,"
becoming marked with
self-centering pride
riding between the fallen tree
and the real tree of life.
Children born
or spawned from a glass tube,
only your Father above
knows the path His children will take
- - -

Young And Old Beware

The only test life has for us
is right here now.
"We have failed too many times
with marks
no one can begin to see,
except garbage and strife
being kicked about like those causes
eating away the insides
of you and me."

Caution I stress in poem
the purpose we seek
I tell you this
from the heart in me
it's true,
creatures formed in
dark places
some having faces or none at all,
but you shall know the last state.

Before you could have
even known
suffering was already there,
in and around you.
We must realize this other character
within,
a greater power of good
is what we must seek
growing sure in solid sequence.

If knowledgeable sight is
achieved,
"the spirit that guides you with emotion
intellect and will,
will share not those scares
that show in the eyes and
actions
of your own brother and sister"

- - -

Mankind's Kind

Brought forth today a gift as it was once
before people forgot the real way
working to benefit their own cause.

Feeling as though this world
I've never really known, like yourselves
learning a part in the thinking process,
figuring you've got all the answers
to the unseen spiritual realm.

You hide your schemes openly
against another person's well being,
while the real secrets are kept away
from what's due you,
for what goes around
comes around
and the suffering will deepen within
your own turf
until you make things right!

"The pain I can take
you have been so gracious to give
the children and me
by taking care of number one,
finding out later
why our families are no longer with good thought
or properly taught,"
in this so-called world of a choked morality
and watered down honesty
from your own behalf of course!

Thanks be it to Him
who has shown us His day
and felt His feeling of love through given time
that said,
"I am with you
who seek Me and my Son"
- - -

Abortion
(neither side is the winner here)

You have one side telling everyone
they're killing innocent babies
instead of bringing them into this coldhearted,
backstabbin', raping,
murdering, jobless, immoral world
ruled by the white devil slavemaster!
Sure, why not,
bring 'em all on in here
the more the merrier,
because misery loves company
around here.

"So what if she doesn't want that child
forced on her
or if she isn't mentally or financially ready,
it doesn't matter.
Let the poor person next door
who's in debt
got four of his own and being taxed
to death
pay a little more,
you know they won't mind!"
Sadly enough
we should understand someday
taking any life is wrong,
the cost being dealt in pain for everyone.

Our concern is to realize the
real issue
no matter which way we turn
to accuse,
people here already know the problem
would not exist
"if the younger and older children
had the <u>decency</u>
keeping to themselves,
before they get their lives together"
- - -

Looking At You

Love is the deepest penetration
of my life's existence
created within
the most perfect Being,
as my mind seems to explore
a life's long dream of love
for what's really there,
which I believe we all can share.

When you feel the warmth of
soul within,
it's there
yet most never see.
People abuse love with little regard
dwelling in thought,
somehow through the course of time
it's left behind.

"Sorrow an' tears are everywhere
in this world
while our blood has flowed too many times
because of greed and thoughtlessness,
we learn
from our own environment today."

The wound has weakened even more
as it seeps into the earth
like an oil spill on a beach,
it's there then gone
but is it?

Through your mind's surroundings
of life
that have always been there
still we neglect to see
what we truthfully should be,
as a people.

(con't)

66

Can you feel it from where
you are,
love is here
and now is the time to let it
be known
you can feel this living in your own heart.

To understand one's love for life
and the need to make things right
is what's important,
(setting ourselves forth on a course
of unity
that will prevail over all colors)

Because we are encircled in our own dreams
of today
tomorrow may never be
what our brothers and sisters are hoping
they'll see.

Looking at you
will help us know ourselves
providing the time is with us in what we do
as one
helping others help themselves.

"For we've traveled the long
hard road
though we have further to go,
let us see
what we can do now,   between us:"
- - -

Where Is This Love

What used to be used to be
today we can make
history.
Right still verses wrong
until the good force shows His hand,
it's always been the plan.

The lifeline was
severed
so choice could be made,
though the sight today is not a
pretty one.

Yes,
the world used to be righteous
and bright as life
it may have been,
"yet nowadays the light has grown
so dim,
leaving us with
the only way out is what's left
within."

If you have listened to the world's
cries
your heart would surely know
the wind has changed,
telling us
it's wrong getting involved before
you should
evils got us thinkin' it's good,
as all it brings down is old weak age
and the truth about sin.

Adam and Eve
ate the forbidden fruit
and cursed one another throughout time

(con't)

with nothing else left
to do,
except being with someone in how we
long to feel,
love's freedom became a
myth
resulting in rape and sick abuse.

We examine the world frame by frame
we bite the bullet and
hide the pain,
leaving us this severed cord
in question,
"of how we get out
before the light darkens
sealing our spirit in;
do ya think the President or congress
know where to begin?"

Given love from above
is where to look,
it's got to be right an' real
if we're ever gonna feel
how it should be.

I like you search an' dream
to find love's answer
hoping to fill the void in our hearts.

"Until we seek the truth
through God
love's severed cord because of two,
will keep rotting our dreams from
becoming true"

- - -

Morality Will Live
(within the children who seek it)

Using our children
to gain
what you must have now,
keeping them from preparing
for the changes ahead
making them weak
dependent on,
"give me this
give me that
and I want this too!"

Though you're too young
to see now
you are being subjected
to the wicked system's ways
thinking it's right,
yet I tell you they're wrong.

As time shows the changes
within the world
you will learn basic lowly needs
to get by,
staying away from
false corrupt thoughts
causing selfish dishonor
people boast of.

Your family knew better
though money spoke louder than
morality,
"forcing them to use you
so everything could be made fast and easier
for them,"
like the five-minute nuked dinner
to the latest cheap fashions
the inflated rich and poor alike

(con't)

68

wallow in.

Children,
unite together
and keep your children safe
from these things
that have made this world the ugly hell
it's becoming,
the hell our fathers and children alike
will bear
when time runs out on them!

"Seek the truth,
you will then know
I have seen you
caught up in our forefathers'
mistakes
being handed down
to us,"
which nobody needs anymore
- - -

You Are His World
(and we must repent and believe)

Lord
Jesus Christ,
our Father Jehovah God
Creator of all things,
"I say unto Thee I am a sinner
in Your eyes
and through those realms
of everything that is You
and Your house,
I have disgraced and
instilled hurt
with unforgettable sorrow."

My tongue
has spoken foul against Thee and
Thy throne,
for the sons of Thine
I have lied, cheated and to
Thy women abused inside.
For this I know not the words
to tell of my sins
rendered
upon Thy children
of Your world.

I can only ask for forgiveness
though I have given Your house nothing
adding to the dirt in the streets.

Difficult as it was
breaking down Your work
into the swirl of poem
hoping to keep away these sins
from Your children
is why I write what I write,
that people may know Your truth

(con't)

before the end comes
ask in my name
to You in Yours,
(for I wish there was no sin found
inside of me)

As a son
I leave You with this small plea
concerning the children
who are seeking You
to be their spiritual guide of truth
will have nothing more to hide.

These string-pulled puppets called
world leaders I disown
who cannot accept the changes that are coming,
as in the spring of
"nineteen hundred and seventy-five
when love's feeling was put into our bowels
by Jehovah God
and felt over all the earth by everyone."

Throughout all of this
the brothers who know
Your will
have found out
You are indeed, very very real
- - -

Sincere Talk
(makes for a closer walk)

While talking with a friend
about many important things
which meant so much
to me and him,
"I realized half way through
he wasn't even listening.
After walking away
he almost made me forget
what we had come together to say."

Is every day like this one
it's true,
after you engage in a conversation
it was anything except
what was supposed to be shared.

Are you reading my words
for what I didn't hear so clear
to remember or express,
on what happens to people
who seek to speak in direction
but are not allowed the real need of existence
in their own life.

Where is this brother
I thought I found today
as we try reaching for this certain kind
of understanding
that seems fleeting at every turn,
"being able to hold on somehow
against all odds in faith
pulling our lost people back up
against me,
for the protection mankind sorely needs."

Our children's future is at stake

(con't)

letting them make their own doom or
freedom.
Fathers tell their families
they love them so,
then off to work destroying us
is where they are.

There isn't much love in this world
because you have neglected
the very purpose that was supposed to be
an important part of life,
"though you will never admit this to yourself,
your children or friends,
but inside there is no escape!"

I know of the insight
you wanted to listen
but not hearing for anyone except who,
yes yes
it has always been us
and never you,
and we know, now that's not true
it's always been you for you!

When the end comes
the blame will rest on those who didn't care,
for we haven't much more time left
to do
before leaving your prison
of blues
- - -

Being In
(but not part of this world)

Isn't this what our companies
are all about,
or the person you work for?
Coasting through life spending up
the profits
faster than you can make it
at your expense,
"forging a blood-filled calendar
is all they've sown my friend
for the reapers
have not the heart they say
and their concern involves only them
today."

Sentencing the blue collar worker
throughout
every back-breakin' day,
until their physical body and spirit give way,
ending up in a state-run
looney-tune center
or on the street in a soup line
with bitter memories and a lot of hidden tears!

Greed for pained labor
makes the material world around you
sing
so you think now,
adding to
the blood-filled calendar
"fixing fate of your blackened soul
that will crush you and the evil one
forever!"

The final days are numbered
within God's time frame,
the workers in the factories wishing

(con't)

they could make a united stand
only to lose what they've gained,
while the companies make the laws
to suit their greedy purpose
causing hardships for those who want
to work.
It all boils down
to the rich man's money plan,
the crooked banking system
and those gutless old people in power!

Therefore, a change of heart
soon to come, there's no other way,
as our calendar will no longer
be crossed off
in hopes of making it through until tomorrow.
With the threat of clouded gloom
pouring from the reaper's hand
weapons of war
raised against the Son of man,
though He will shield you
from this whiplash-like tragedy
of ignorance and horror.

The meek numbers many
as our calendar calls out once again
to be cleansed;
telling us
"never have you seen or gone the right way
but you will see and feel the pain
of the last day,
when Jesus carts you so-called
big shots and know-it-alls
away!"
- - -

The Gay Side
(it's nowhere)

Children
of the inflicted diseases,
hear my words.
When you were young
feeling your way about,
your parents and family members
outsiders too,
made you accept their wrong desires.

"While this was happening
you had no way to know or
turn,
now you're older
it's all you think is right."

Know,
when a person is the same likeness
boy or girl
it matters not,
except realizing it's wrong
for anyone to be feeling your
body over
forcing themselves on or into you,
nor you them.
Being rejected
is enough hurt mentally
by the opposite mate,
but it doesn't mean there's something
wrong with you.

Though seeking another avenue
trying to get even,
doing your act with someone
who isn't sure about his feelings
when you know better,
"the evil one is there

(con't)

72

laughing
at the both of you!"

The Lord Thy God Almighty
says it's wrong
His Word tells you so,
for He is pure, Holy
and will not justify
a man loving another man
a woman loving another woman
of any age,
or men looking like women
women acting like men;
doing those immoral things
leading to your
disgrace!

Hear my warning,
if you continue
to use others for your vile pleasures
then feel the pain of suffering
come upon you
like you never dreamed possible,
guaranteeing your life
won't be so dull and boring
while you struggle near the end, to stay alive;
after death
finding your reward for living the blind lie!

- - -

Talk Freely To Me, I'm Listening

Talk freely to me, I'm listening
I want to know
what you have to say.
You've found out they're persecuting
me and you,
slowly taking our rights away.

They're so busy scheming
to bring the revenue their way
they've forgotten you my friend,
although that's not the impression
they leave you with
leading up to election day.

"Seeing the multitude jobless, starving
homeless
rejected by selfish people
both glaring back at me,
though I have an answer
but no means to see it through
without you."

I feel your thoughts
burning into my heart
what you want to say,
like what good am I to you
or what good are you to me;
well they've kept us this way!

Talk freely to me, I'm listening
I want to know
what you have to say.
To learn their secrets of worthless
promises:
depriving, disguising, analyzing
for themselves.

(con't)

Are you going to keep
being taken in,
doesn't anyone want to grasp
the left hand of truth and win?

Have you asked them
what it is they hide,
"looking like full of grace
the forked-tongued demon
will soon arrive
and the material stamp of the beast
is what you will be forced to buy!"

Talk freely to me, I'm listening
I want to know
what you have to say.
I've heard talk an' more talk
from both sides,
though there's nothing coming
our way.

They sneak around making laws
to protect their interests
turning the children and working people
into believing they're inferior, expendable
when they're really okay.

It's the evil force around us
they used
to keep us apart,
though it wasn't me or you
in years gone by
that degraded or hurt one another.

"But this force,   still
turning the cities and towns
into sleazier slums
feeding on you day after day
keeping everyone bitter
so peace will never come!

Unless you change your heart
our souls will remain captive, father to son"
- - -

In The Year 3070

I'll finally have a job
I can oversee
checking on the fire
and safety
of the ones who
turned away,
from what they heard and knew
to be the truth in life,
why!

I've been told
there will be many souls
like grains of sand
covering the seashore
being persuaded to leave
righteousness
following darkness into the
lake of fire,
why!

"What more is there than
being happy, free
inheriting a joyous world of peace and
love,
for you well know
there isn't any other need
we need
more meaningful in life itself."

You're not blind anymore;
we all know what we've been through
in the last world,
(B.C. to 2000 A.D.)
Seeing and feeling the horrors
which devastated this entire earth until
God and Jesus
ended our heavy suffering for a time.

(con't)

The wind-blown darts of sin
will manifest again
when the devil is freed for a
short while,
today's society should remember
one tends to think the grass is greener
on the other side,
yet you reach there
finding you should have stayed
where you were.

"Until you come full circle with the Lord
thy God,
you will never hold insight to anything
spiritual."

So will it be at the end
of the millennium-reign's search,
reaping what you have sown
causing your own eternal pain
for falling asleep in
church.

Know before you get tricked
into believing his lie,
there's no grass at all
where the deceiver takes you, to the other
side!
When our loving Father brings
the evil ones
to their final judgement,
in what has to be
will be done, swiftly
- - -

It Takes Two To Reach There
(and it works both ways)

Why is it one always can see
while the other sees only when it's convenient?
Dwelling on those words
you used to say,
wondering why none of them
was meant for you or me.
"Just enough said to get us by
until we ran out of things
to say and do."

I hoped the differences
we were having would lessen
though the hype and position offered
meant more,
prior to reaching there
things between us crumbled into
despair.

I try to tell myself
our love should have been enough,
but your feelings turned
to stone
for me and things inside the home,
like those passive bad habits
we did without thinking
would have never gotten in our way
while you made it to wherever you are today.

Okay,
you have your education, position
and all the money you need baby
though isn't it a shame,
"you've made all new friends
now you think everything's cool
your ol' man's name forgotten,
wow
what a fool!"
- - -

Jews For Jesus

I couldn't speak any words
at that moment,
just walking around
keeping the joy inside
with no one to talk to,
when I first heard about
Jews for Jesus.

"Long, long ago, a blessing was given
the chosen people of Israel,
a covenant
from the Living God."
Now more and more it blossoms
like a wild flower near the water's edge
as Jew and Gentile step forward
accepting the old destroyed scriptures from
the hands an heart of Jesus.

(There really are Jewish people
who weren't fooled,
knowing Christ is aligned
with the fine woven thread that's held us
all together
since His death and resurrection)
The 2000-year span of tears and time
has been a living nightmare
no aware soul can deny!

Through the evil brainwashed thoughts of
Lucifer
many of you have believed.
For the remaining remnant of Israelites
and Gentiles alike,
"I kneel
holding out my hand to you
saying,
you're special within me"
- - -

There's Got To Be Another Way
(for you and me)

You say you like me
later on
I say I love you,
but how can I trust
in what I feel
until I know for sure?
Guess I will have to pretend
a little while longer.

How much heartache
before we know
what we've felt and what we'll feel
will remain with us,
"for the world is so wrong
yet looks so right
it's affecting me and you,
taking away the little things
that brought us our smiles and tears
we've shared."

Wherever I am
when I look to my left
or to my right
will you be there
near me,
or will I always walk alone?

"Pretending comes easier when
through the years
everybody uses you up like a sponge
until the hurt doesn't squeeze out
anymore,"
making it harder to reach out
one for another
when we can sense this love
being implanted

(con't)

77

in our hearts,
knowing
it is the real deal for us.

I say I like you
later on
you say you love me,
but how can you trust
in what you feel
until you know for sure?

Guess the both of us will have to pretend
an' hang on
a little while longer,
"though I can't speak for you
but I really don't want to pretend,
anymore"
- - -

I'm Searching For You
(the prisoner)

Whoever has an ear
let him listen,
if you have a heart
carry the dream until we meet.

We cannot travel this road alone
so dig deep inside along the way,
give those who wish it the truth
waste not your time who refuse.
Been wondering how you're doin'
for a day doesn't pass
I'm worrying about you.

"Look back, look ahead,
remember the kind of life you've led
and what you want to do differently
once you're released,
before you're dead."

As we press on
darkness finds its prey
luring us in
until the next thing ya know
we're doin' time for a crime
we thought we'd gotten away with.

"Watching the vile majority consumed with
hate, drugs, alcohol, pride and violent schemes,
keeps you backsliding further away
from the ones you love
and the ones who loved you
for what you were,   before you changed."

Don't keep feeding off the
evil spirit,
open up your eyes and see

(con't)

love's trying to break through
before there's nothing left of you!
If you're not ashamed of what
you have become
it will certainly cost your family and friends,
long before your stretch is done.

Look,
what happened happened
you're where you are and it's
done now,
though you can turn yourself around
walking away from it all,
you've got to want to make the call.

I need and love you
and I didn't write this to pressure
your stride
I just want you to walk out alive;
for there's much work that needs to begin
but I could use a little help
from a friend.

Though you ask Him
for real
it will be given anew,
you can make it through
if you would only believe in you
and the One who forgives, if ya want to
- - -

Cremation

You speak of the spirit
yet you take up the space
of another breath.
The land
showing signs of no place
to play or run,
should tell enough to one.

Throwing down life
to lifeless light on them
taking away their vision,
professing in the One
who can do everything
while being lowered into what?
Just to look again
at another fading cold stone!

The element of change
pressing against our inner core
chewing the struggle
right out of us,
keeps our brain-washed minds
"from seeing
it's the memory and spirit
that's needed,
passing it along for our families' sake
through time."

Listen closer to the real song
of this world;
"through dirt to life
as breath was given
though death to ashes,
it is true
spirit born
will be taken back to our Heavenly Father

(con't)

79

where you will then see."

Remember the way they were
which is tough enough to handle sometimes
by not going back
or not wanting to look back
hurting when you do,
wishing there was another way
you could break through to reach them
making sure they're okay.

Hoping to see them again we wonder
all the time,
even though
to soften your helpless fears
of right then
you know you never will,
(until later)

Still,   you take up the space of
another breath
- - -

The Written Word
(all of it)

Churches around the world
preach your Holy Word
which suits their feelings,
refusing what the
twelve brothers gave us,
neglecting spiritual growth and healing
of our broken hearts.

When will we learn
it never comes out right
when we don't listen?
Is this Word we read
not the same
always thinking it says something
different
instead of what's really there?

Being brought up under certain
doctrines,
is this our only near-sighted goal;
"or is it the whole Word of God
that's needed,
to shoot the light of truth and
understanding
into a darkened soul?"

All I'm asking Jesus
is keep us aware,
"without losing your faith in love
falling back into darkness
from saving grace,
having our names blotted out from the
Lamb's Book of life
is what's at stake."

There are many you call

(con't)

oh Lord,
but few are chosen
because their works are not of You.
Let us know through Your will
who truly means well
that we're able to tell.

It's only You, Brother Jesus
destroying my weary fears
speaking to Your Father's children
through the remainder of our cosmic
eternal years.

Forging us to be strong
yet humble in life
needed to beat the artificial strife
encamped on all sides,
though evil will never burst in and win
because Jesus is there
threshing the threshing floor,
backed by
(the spring of living water
flowing from its core,
yes
the Creator of life
for ever ever more)
- - -

Freedom's Reality

Freedom
through spiritual measure
of a human being's worth is scaled equally
by God.

In this world without God
freedom is secretly given
to a few,
(while others dream of it
but will never know to hold
this precious gift)

We keep wasting time
and time is wasting us,
seems kind of creepy, spooky
this love we need and
long for.

Some are lucky
learning they have only to ask,
though others will not listen
turning themselves, their surroundings
into trash.

"Wanting the key
freeing up your heart and mind,
loosening those chained feelings
so the soul can flow out from
being confined."

I ask myself what's He's doing
up there,
it's all that love is supposed
to be.
We look for justice but it's not here
like it should be
and people tell you:

(con't)

"Don't worry
things will be better tomorrow,"
well that's my fear
thinking, will it ever reach here,
except these strange-looking cult people
claiming to be the heir.

I'm always wondering how I or anyone
could know the real side of life
before we leave
because everything's closing in on
the children an' me!

We keep wasting time
and time is wasting us,
seems kind of creepy, spookie
this love we need and
long for.

I'll keep on searching until we stand
together
leanin' against the great door,
that the Lord might reach through
bringing us into this
truest love,
fulfilling our empty dream
called freedom

- - -

A Bluesman's Song

Many many times I've wondered
and worried about the children's path
they choose to follow,
while the blues overwhelm my heart
my outgoing spirit
I can't hang onto anymore,
when I'm feelin' hollow.

I'm needin' someone to look up to
showing me what to do
making it worth everything,
tomorrow.

"The blues make me sense
our earthly walk
keeping me humble, low
on an' even keel,
where everyone will realize
when the blues sweeps down through
into their unworthy soul
until we reach the one true goal."

It was the blues from the beginning
man could only pay
feeling the persecution and hardships
of being walked on every day
thinking their life was useless,
some surely knew
an outlet of sounds would help them
through,
forging their deep roots
few are blessed to play.

Later
creating a cheap fleshy pleasure
that never satisfies or teaches the way
many of the younger brothers,

(con't)

82

black and white
filed the blues away.

Life is felt through big and small
the blues breaks down the enemy's
wall,
and lightens my battered soul
while I wait for the children
to open their eyes
seeing it all,
(filling me with your hope and peace, Lord
being of one accord;
it's the only thing left, I can afford)

As the end times touch our lives
there's no disguise,
having less an less fun
there's no tuning
it out
hiding, or no place to run.

People will be crying throughout every land
being cursed
for choosing the wrong way,
while those blues roll around here
once again
reminding you why they're here today;
though in reality they never were
too far away.

"God knows where all of us have been
dwelling in the root of
David,
nothing will ever change my heart
nothing will tear us apart,
nothing will lure us astray
or destroy our gifted melody,
for the Lord hears, His chosen play"
- - -

Memory

Memory itself
seems torn between thoughts
not knowing the real direction,
so we make up our own
telling others around us.
Some
you have given in trust
answers to questions we summon
are forthcoming.

"Knowledge will rekindle the
embattled subconscious
inside your head,
clearly seeing the spiritual war
that's destroying our lands
our people,
before we're dead."

Conquest over the Christians is written
for a short while.
"Those left behind finally seeing the truth
will repent
changing their ways,"
thinking they would never see
the day
where they could do a little more
than make ends meet,
only to realize during the onslaught
they should have listened to that person
who shared, then left with grief.

When God's wrath enters
this world,
a terrifying piercing scream will sound
in the sinner's ear,
hearing victory's call with judgement
sealed

(con't)

riding the vast space of time,
healing our memories of yesterday
without anymore crime.

Though presently fighting
evil desires
to regain earth's honorable balance,
our hearts pouring into one another
like a raging river
never going away empty,
or thirsty.

If you truly wish to drink like Christ did
from the same cup
to learn what's up
you must push aside the old attitude
an' trigger the new,
to reframe from being an ungrateful
pup.

From dark days to righteous ways
in light
you can win the inner fight
to keep life's memory alive
throughout eternity we will strive,
going with the flow
in love
provided by
God and His Blessed Jesus;
just thought you'd like to know
- - -

People Just Talk To Talk
(and never do or say anything)

Many speak
of how they're somebody
but the world they live in
is nowhere to be
found.

"Talk is cheap
and everyone has learned how
to run his mouth,
finding out later they think about
what should have been said,
after it cost 'em."

You talk about how bad you are
in what you do
showing off, humiliating
when there's no need,
boasting you will be the bad man
until the bad man comes.

"To enlighten ya,
I wish I could have told it
to your face,
but it isn't me
and brother,   it isn't you!"

If you don't change and
gett yourself, your place in order
you're gonna wake up
a hurtin' unit.

I know the Brother who's
coming back
"where every good and evil knee
will bow
an' tongue confess,
because He is
bad to the bone"
- - -

Is It Always Going To Be Goodbye

Everyone's saying goodbye
though I say hello
must you or I
say goodbye
while trying to express our feelings
of one another?

Should either of us
walk away
if we keep within
how we first came to know
why
we say hello,
"never wanting to remember
what goodbye means
people say what they do."

Please,
don't tell me goodbye
is all that any of us
here
has left to give
- - -

Magic Carpet

Oh magic carpet on the floor
rise up, rise up
I'll tell you more.
Yes it's time
so hurry, hurry be quick,
I need you to reach
the distressed and the sick.

Oh magic carpet you're all I have
I'm counting on you
traveling through life's narrow path,
you might reach my people
before they stumble and crash.
With my heart next to yours
I know you know
I made and hold the keys
of life and death,
for the children choosing you
will fly free.

"To touch the magic within your hand
breaths of life
sweeping over every land
snatching from the fire,
show them
that they may know I'm no liar."

Oh magic carpet
where is tomorrow's day;
we've learned your lesson
now show us the way.
Hearing about those three wishes
from the magic lamp
you would surely give,
"after everything you asked of me
I've done,
I see you have granted all three
in one"

- - -

The Airplane Ride

The airplane movie was funny
indeed,
though hearing about reality
turned tragedy over our skies
while we figure out why.
"The nerve endings of your
airtraffic controllers
must be split a hundred ways
by time's end of their horrifying day,
like the half-dazed pilot avoiding a near
miss,
spilling sweat and fear
on whoever is near."

The highjackers are a weird
sick breed
playing the deadly game,
thinking why should I risk death
when we can slip a bomb on board
fatally destroying innocent people,
while chanting victory with their
ungodly friends
over another lost cause.

It's not like it used to be
the big bird
cruisin' 33 thousand feet
500 miles an hour at a peaceful ease,
then oh,   "the sudden heavy turbulence
cracks ripping down the seams,
pieces of the plane being
blown away
right before your eyes:"
You're sitting there all shook up
ready to scream
hoping to reach your destination thinking,
this is got to be some kind of a real
mad dream!
- - -

Waiting For Truth

Paying the price
suffering all kinda ways
breaking down mentally and physically
wishing it would go away,
every hurt feelin'
every fear
every stained-dried tear
trying to be heard,
"dealing with pin-heads
who control with greed,
and oh,   so quickly the hour cometh
they will be on their knees,   begging
like we had to beg!"

Their system
they figure, has all the needs
slashing each other's throat
with a deadly smile,
when your back is turned
they squirm to survive!
Yeah,
that's the real corporate dream
knowing there's nothing we can do
to stop them,
they run off to other countries, destroying
their lands while raking in huge profits.

However this reminder we keep inside
tells us,
"vengeance belongs to One
I know
and oh,   so quickly the hour cometh
they will be on their knees,   begging
to the extreme,
and nobody's going to care about their
useless screams!"
- - -

My Personal Flavor

All my life I've been a sinner
doin' things I knew
and didn't know were wrong,
but lately Lord Jesus
I'm beginning to look to you
for the first time.
"I finally see this attitude of mine
the way I was raised
kept me away
from the spiritual truth in you."

I'm trusting the children will catch
your meaning
staying pumped up and primed,
while we fight to protect
their innocence
building up our Father's kind.
"When I was hurting deep inside
there was no one around to scrape me
off the floor
'til I believed about you Lord,
realizing then
there you were all the time
workin' to save my life."

There are a lot of different ways
we're led to go
and many I've tried,
but lately Lord Jesus
I'm beginning to look to you
for the first time,
because you opened up my eyes
revealing the hidden disguise
between the spiritual truth and the devil's
glazed-over lies.
Like cake and ice cream,
you're my personal flavor
and I'll love you always for it,   Lord
- - -

Life's Second Chance

Life's giving never tends to know
true worth
we take for granted,
until a brush with death happens.
Suddenly this precious
second chance
and your whole life changes.

Don't waste this new insight
you've gained,
"don't just say you're gonna do
things differently
settling back into your old ways
throwing away your first and maybe
last chance,
changing for the better."

However,
there are many who can never tell
or show anyone they love the difference
for escape was impossible,
"while suffering
never really leaves family members
and friends who survive."

Don't think they were alone
as life's spiritual force
hidden from us mortals is with them,
if they reached out with faithful hope
before darkness closed in.

The agony over death flees
for it cannot enter the sacred place,
"while that special piece of you
in love
goes freely with their spirit
where the avenger waits to comfort,
and one day, even the score!"

- - -

The Secrets We Carry

There's a story in every soul
who walks by you
and you them.

Ever wonder
what they've been through,
what they know
what special gift they hold?

Everyone is hurt, angry
thirsting for righteousness
in our wake of waiting.

"Through all these things we have
endured
while bits and pieces of our life
crumble within
the older we get."

The last generation with little working
faith
feeling empty, forgotten.
Could it really be us this time around
do you feel it is?

While we struggle past Armageddon's
strain
with great battles
filled with victories and sorrows,
fought by those gifted people who were
obedient to God
through their inflicted pain of yesterday,
shall behold this lost garden
in the holy land
throughout the millennial reign

- - -

The Big Ladle

Mr. Mandela,
your people
like many other tribes
have suffered so long,
and your prayers
have not been in vain.

The power of God
will fall on their wicked hidden
racist hearts
soon to come brother,
"and freer you all shall be
if the brothers would only give their
hand an' heart as one
to each other,   in trust
there would be no more hurting nation."

May this love you have for
life
fill up the big dipper
in the sky
so we can pour it out
onto the world,
that people will know the need
is clear
for all colors and creeds
of man,
together now in one atmosphere
- - -

One Two Three
(why is it we can't see)

It's because of You Father
You are number One,
for the left arm
of Your glorious power holds and guides
the strong right arm
of Your only begotten Son.

Though many people, Christians too
can't accept You as You
and Your Son Jesus as two,
the Holy Spirit through an' through.

Given visions I've seen from You
concerning Your Son,
all three could call upon
Your splendor
and become as one
- - -

How Long

How long before you realize
if ever the spiritual way?
How long before the ice melts
thawing to care besides yourself?
How long before the hate you store up
for someone is forgiven?

"How long before anything anyone
who was ever good, had a say
and it touched you so that you
listened
and made the effort in your life?"

How long before we agree in faith
over someone's well being,
their message.
How long before we move
getting involved that God might
guide us?

How long before we find some good things
from the different religions,
putting them to use in our own walk?

How long will it be
tell me, tell me
what it's going to take to make you see?
How long before you know what it is
I've got to do to get through
make up my mind why don't ya,
it's not just the earth an' you
there's other people living here too!

How long before you start checking out
the real scene,
"for life is dying because of little
self-centered
feel-nothing you!"
- - -

Love's Calling

I want to see your ability
to love,
I want to hear your softness
of words in love.

Will your heart be warm always
to touch in love,
"as our feelings swell
within us
keeping our souls adrift some where
in wedlock,
is how it should be.
Guess we both wish
all these things were found in
our love."

If you truly loved
would we lose our youth
and vows we eagerly make
watching life blossom then fade
like the day,
oh,   this love
has surely gone astray.

To hold love's yearning
we must submit together,
quit running those
sweet little nothings whispered,
turning the lying and cheating
into our every day normal burning.

Maybe then
this love we feel and hate to
leave
will always be,
no matter the distance or time
we're apart
- - -

My Last Peace

Often I think how I could share
with you
that you would see,
knowing today it's easy being
deceived.

"Many people, their different ways
never lasting but awhile
wondering where they'll be headed
after the trial,
once we've crossed the finish line
of the marathon's last mile?"

We're so desperate to find an answer
for our woes
we start believing in our foes,
or not at all
until our back is pinned against the wall
and we're on our way out
seeking the Lord then,
while we fall.

Get guts enough to face yourself
you've got to want it,
reaching within before you can straighten out
keeping it in,
(because everybody's patience
is wear'n kinda thin nowadays)

No other way left
my last peace in hope
written for you and yours to be,
answering truth with blessings of a
loving spirit
we all long to see.

Forming a blend

(con't)

96

of religious and secular worth
so you can realize the two are
showing you
much of the same things,
"focusing on life, these feelings we feel
through our families and friends
where we've been,
where we're going
while we choose what's right,
we've got to reach the one true light."

Or will it be you
facing His angry might
spending an eternity of horrified nights,
being banished from
His sight?

"The younger generation
into a physicial fitness thing
working hard to exercise the body
and discipline the mind
keeping the muscles fit and strong,
you must also work to purify your heart
through the spirit
every day
discerning right from wrong."

Concerning this spiritual faith
in hope through belief
there's no other way,
it is what feeds and heals you
inside,
pulling us through this dark lonely
unforgiving plight
- - -

Life's Real Fragrance

Keep those soft-colored petals
of spring
I've gathered,
take them wherever you go.
While many let loose all reasoning of
truth
there is nothing we can do,   except
reach for those soft-colored petals
to remember
the sweet scent of spring,
that will awaken this world
once again
- - -

A Fool In Thought

People laugh knowing the truth
of why it had to be this way.
I have no mind I can claim like you
as you first thought,
being shown visions through Him
you saw the difference.

I've been disliked by many spiritual beings
around earth's creation you cannot see
with your eyes alone,
getting to the root of our problems
where many are prone!

"Brought up under a certain doctrine
disregarding the rest of
God's Holy Word,
was your biggest mistake my blind brother.
You never made the effort to find the whole truth
and Jesus isn't gonna buy your
lame excuse!

You know who you are and never
will I be like you here.
You've undermined His treasure
utilized these measures
and for years this struggle
has been caused by the likes of you!

You aim your sights toward heaven
yet it won't even be
by the skin of your teeth,
inside you're nothin' but a cheat.

"Realize the pain an' grief you've caused others
being led by the nose, with a plank in your eye,
I can see through your disguise!"
For I've known a long time
I've been nothing to you

- - -

The Fighter
(inside the squared circle)

I overheard one champion say
he really didn't know why
he was fighting.
After becoming the champ
and liking the money and publicity,
were the only two advantages he saw
for such a grueling, bloody sport.

I smiled somewhat knowing his thoughts
concerning the spiritual change,
hitting us
like a flurry of powerful blows
to the body!

"When tomorrow brings this
great event,
the brothers that made it inside
the squared circle
to those who didn't fare as well,
will be side by side, engaged in war
against the evil destroyer of man,
which is the main battle plan."

If you're searching for truth
realize the One who has made you,
bringing life and respect back into
this world
along with freedom too,
(something we all wish we had
not just a few)

"We will be forever
under His watchful eyes
and the rebellious lot who's out of control,
will find out soon enough
why they call it a TKO
in the boxing world"
- - -

Feel The Trade Winds Blowin'
(all around us)

I'm going to catch that breeze
outa' here,
our spirits lifting together
until we reach where we should be
by following Your lead, Lord.

Look out jet stream here we come
tradin' in our old self
being made like new
lighter than air through transformation
feeling the presence of You,
carrying us up
into that beautiful place
with plenty of graceful space
- - -

The Message

Future lines written
many have spoken
a word or more of guidance,
showing a way
to listen and read,
applying it for the good of man.

What difference is this
picture,
expressing guarantees
evolving to what will be,
(not what we have become
that we try not to see)

Holding unknown power way outa' sight
coming soon against the evil ones
who think they rule
the day and night,
should serve as a warning to ya.

Helping the ones who need
taking those necessary steps forward
releasing
the enslaved heart and soul,
"implementing love
of the message given
those capable of brotherhood,
to be edified within all
who do these works of truth"
- - -

Be Born Again
(of water and the Holy Spirit)

(From light,
for light
to light,
is life)

If you miss the rapture
it means
you didn't repent and
believe
the given word of our
Lord Jesus
and must lay down your life;
"if the devil catches you"
to gain true sight
of our
heavenly Father an' Son's fight,
taking this world back
from the cold-hearted night
- - -

Can't Forget You

I've looked back a little ways
and tried to remember you,
but with so much on
my mind
I'm forgetful sometimes.

Wherever I turn
when something is goin' down
that matters,
there we are in what we've done
finally getting through,
in how our thoughts
of not too often, seem to be.

Remembering you
through all those times
we spent together
is what I need from you.

"Now that all of us have to go our
different ways
I can barely find my happiness
until yes,
through you
in my thoughts
it keeps me strong enough,
being caught downwind
withstanding the gale-force winds."

The second my fears
creep their way
before I almost lose it,
thoughts of you
come flowing back inside
of me
breaking the swell to calm,
as I've looked back

(con't)

103

a little ways
I was able to remember you,
helping me through another tough moment.

Time you say
you wish we had,
even though it takes away
the reasons
for all those things
we just didn't have the time
to do,
though we felt one another's feelings
sharing life's destined plan.

Whatever happens tomorrow
"it's what you stand for,
I'll never forget
what you mean to me,"
in how our thoughts
of not too often, seem to be

- - -

My-tray-ah

Rumor has it
you came descending to earth
from on a cloud in Kenya, Africa,
confronting a prayer vigil of five thousand souls.

Being amazed at this feat
and worshiping you as Jesus Christ,
you didn't rebuke them
because you're another one of those
wanna be's,
but you haven't got what it takes
my man!

You left for London, England,
where you've been staying
since dropping in on us, about 1977
which is the lowest part under heaven.

Making many predictions
some have come true
though many, like the Gulf War
never came through for you,
which means your cover's blown
your respect I disown
as the elect of God know
you're just another demon
sent from Lucifer to deceive the weak
in spirit.

My Father's Holy Word states in Matthew
24:24 and 24:30
the truth about Jesus when He returns,
as every eye shall see Him
not just a handful.

You do not hold the key to life
the power, or light

(con't)

as does my Father in heaven
along with the real Son of man,
who is yet to come.

Woe be to you My-tray-ah
for the evil one hasn't a
clue,
when Jehovah's gonna hit 'em;
and after coming to
you, the beast, Lucifer, his demons
and those who follow,
will be cooking up in hell
like a big pot of stew
paying your dues,   forever!
- - -

Have You Seen Me

If I could talk to you
this is what I'd say:
"In my thoughts
I'm hoping someone
will find me,
I'm frightened
wondering what they're going to do
with me."

Wish there was some way I could
call out for help
that you would hear
and reach me,
so I can go back home
and grow up happy like you.
Mommy, Daddy
they've taken me away
from you!

If I could talk to you
this is what I'd say:
"I'm not looking forward to this hurt
I'm feeling
that these spineless people
are putting me through."

"Please hurry, I'm lost
begging,   screaming inside my
tiny little world
for you to care about me,
what else can I do,
don't let them keep taking me
further away from you!"
Oh,
by the way
I love you
Mommy and Daddy
- - -

105

Everyone Wants To Be A Winner
(but reaching there isn't easy)

Oh, the tears and rain,
I hear and feel them both tonight
though lately,
it's coming down so hard
I'm not sure which is which.

Something came to my spirit
pushing its way down deep
crashing through the inner most part
of my heart
the other day,
making me hurt a little more with worry.

"I prayed to Jesus that He would reveal
this heartache of pain,
breaking me into a thousand pieces
all over again."

I won't lose sight of
what's right
pushing back the pressure
standing on God's Word
in hope through faith, this truth I've found.

Keep me steadfast Lord God
against the backlash
of doubt
while seeking the light of life
that sets mankind free,
"is where I hope to find,   you and me
when this trip's over for real,
guess that's what being a winner is
when we see who's carrying God's
true seal"
- - -

The Children
(will they ever listen)

Sometimes
I'd like to think I knew where
to lead the children,
so they would be safe from
any more harm.

Talk to them in such a way
they could sense I cared for them,
maybe trust me enough
seeing together
we've got to be the light in the darkness
for the other children
who live their lives with little care,
little belief,   little love.

"Because few grown-ups really listen,
only a handful can see
what the children can't express in
words
right away,
when they feel the need."

It's just that
I,
I don't want the children to bend too far
an' tear,
wondering when they will come forward
and care
giving their spirit a fighting chance
to shine through,
is why they're worse off for wear
- - -

Be My Valentine

Roses are sweetly scented
lushes
and pulsating red,
while those tiny violets
are the deepest shade of crushed
velvet blue.
Wishing you were near
is all I touch and feel inside
when I dream,
giving my heart to you.

There isn't another girl
anywhere
who could compare,
having a warm sincere heart
and believes in God
like you,
"is why I'm so crazy in love
never wanting us to be through"

XOX   (smile)
- - -

Vengeance Is Mine
(saith the Lord)

You've done all the damage
you could do
now the hour is reaching for you
and there's no place left to hide,
being convicted in the light.

My eyes are focused
my heart ready without a sigh,
I can picture the place and conditions
under which you and your demons
are gonna fry!

"You sneak
your way inside the children's minds
then their hearts
and when you've finished trashing
everything of value and honor,
quietly flying away searching for another
innocent child,
leaving those scars and tears in your wake
before the child catches on
it's too late."

There is an answer, people;
for I know the healer
the One who gives the gift of forgiveness freely
once you believe.

It's You Lord Jesus
You always make things right,
as darkness moves away
from where You tread
day or night,
while You work putting Your Father's children
back together again.

(con't)

You knew before the beginning
of the world
who was going to be a part of Your
beautiful family,
though I fear the worst if people
won't listen.

The darkness has no way out
their fate sealed in hell forever
and the devil is trying to drag you down
with him.

They continue snaring the children along
with lies
immoral lust and the latest song,
keeping everyone's carnal mind busy
until it's too late to change.

The problem is, people don't take Jesus
out of their heads
and bring Him down into
their hearts,
until the children wake up dead
yeah, that's the heavy part!

"Unless you let Jesus do the
fixin',
it's your only guarantee
growing up in God's world,
making you strong enough
so you can find room,   to breathe"

- - -

Is It Too Much To Ask

Many people in the world
are faced with pressing problems
nearing the end of their rope,
ready at any given second
to explode.

You're on the breaking edge
and if you can't hold back the rage
from freaking out on someone
for whatever the reason,
only causes another craze.

Don't flip out, blowing your cool
though its easier said than done,
for the people we hurt will make us later
regret
playing the fool.
When you're hurting inside
it's tough to reach outside,
you think there's no one there who can deal
with you
but it's not true.

While the turmoil builds
day to day, year after year
we become like a walking time bomb,
ready at any given second
to explode, that's everyone's fear.

While you're out there trying to maintain
believe me
we're feelin' each other's strain,
and I want to be there for you
seeking the help you need
through professional people near by,
who are willing to work
charging their ever-increasing fees

(con't)

110

the poor can't afford;
is why we carry the sickness around
seeking other means to set our anger free,
ready at any given second
to explode!

"Life means nothing when you're
torn up inside
never yielding the right of way,
thinking your problems will be history
once you expel your rage
as the mind falls deeper into decay,
you hope nobody crosses
your path today."

Finally it comes to a point
you lose control.
Afterwards,
when you do, it's too late to see
there's nothing left;
you take your own life next.

There is another way of healing
the soul,
"but you keep putting it off
driving yourself crazy
fighting alone,
suffering this agonizing pain
until you fold."

Someone is near
waiting for you to say
a little prayer
making the odds a bit more fair.

You won't have to freak out
throwing everything you've ever hoped
or worked for away,
God's ready at any given second
to change the situation
you've gotten yourself into
an' heal you today

- - -

Earth Day
(awaiting the changes)

Growing up in this world
you wonder what it is
you want to be,
"wishing we could know to see
our choice
ahead of time,
along with the outcome."

As time moves on our interests split
mistakes are made on what to do,
while the earth's air
land and drinking water dwindle
into a hazardous state for many countries;
people telling every one they've got
the answers
but nobody can solve anything,
not even the flu.

We must work together now
saving this environment
changing our priorities before it's too late,
starting with big corporate businesses
whose only interests lie in their
life style first,
through the millions they profit each year
off the poor people,
living from paycheck to paycheck!

Heart-felt concerns shared by
the world
are pressing health problems
like the garbage sites that are nearly filled,
along with those toxic waste dumps
made by federal and civilian companies,
or our nuclear-radiation waste storage problem
which nobody wants in his back yard.

(con't)

The forests are being destroyed
at an alarming rate
with little being done to preserve them.

Many families are affected
through what's being made at certain factories
while claims are brought forth
because of suffering ill health, even death.

"Company employees cover up the problems
and pay out some money when forced to
in keeping the peace,
while denying the truth
as nothing is ever proved.
"
Why is it this way and what can
be done,
when all we have left is one person
bringing a pail of water to a
five-alarm fire.

Yes, it takes money and people
willing to work for a liveable wage
with funding from the federal and state levels
that nobody wants to part with.

The people that can do something
look the other way
or can't be reached for comment
when they're confronted with the blame,
as we sit back and watch our earth day's decline
a little more every year
until we end up killing ourselves,   is, what it is.

"The people responsible for this major
travesty
are lower than
low down dirty dirt,
paying the ultimate price
when they're through entertaining their
fantasy
of a lavish lifestyle, living for Oscar night,
becoming the world's biggest jerk!"

- - -

The Bluesman's Blues

Gazing through your life's
window,
telling anyone who will listen
about your problems that never go away
by hour's end each day,
while tomorrow brings us more of the same ol'
junk mail
nobody cares about.

Our earthly parents in the beginning
had no reason to feel the blues of sorrow
until evil had its way,
committing the first deception
of murdering Abel,
is why we've got those moods
called blues today.

"In healing our situation
just Prophets sent from God
though changing our lifestyle from sin
was too much to ask
to begin,
people in power destroyed the Prophets
as they saw fit."

The sorrow runs deep into our souls
like the unsaved rebels who refuse to
awaken
are headed for the pit,
fearing no power of the Living Spirit
concerning our fold, their life's path is already told.

We're all caught up in this minority complex
"while everybody's bellyachin' and cryin'
in his beer
or whatever it is you drink,
wanting those dreams of freedom and identity

(con't)

112

to be upheld in this melting pot
someone called earth."

The ethnic groups
pushing resentment and barriers on
one another
when reaching out to shake the hand
of the white devil slavemaster,
(you feel the struggle and sorrow
of your families' lives,   run up your arm
injecting the pain,   all over again!)

"Our blues combined is but a drop
in a bucket
compared to God's,
when Lucifer wasted His only Son on
Calvary
for you and me,
reconnecting the door, a gift of life."

As I look through my broken window
it's killin' me too,
there's only so much a few of us
can do.

You brothers haven't the guts to stand up
fighting the real blues
within,
caring and healing for one another every day
"letting our Father in heaven know
we forget Him not,
is why
the blues will always pour
through my head and heart oh Lord."

(No, I won't forget what
Jesus means
through the stretch of road
I've got to go.
Your shed blood in love
came to me from above,
and it finally seeped through, Lord
turning me around,   into you)

- - -

Where There's Smoke There's Fire

There are a lot of different ways
we try
sharing with you,
hoping you would slow down long enough
in the fast lane and listen.

How many more times must you be
reminded
before life flows into your heart
escaping the flames,
causing those emotions of yours
you run with every day
by not repenting of your sin,
is why destruction of the wicked
will soon begin.
"Where there's smoke there's fire!"

We're asking you not to delay any longer
your body only gets weaker
as time goes on
while the evil spirits remain strong.

It becomes harder for you to realize
you're no match for them
without help,
as it may cost you everything you are.
When you see the smoke surround you
know,
"where there's smoke there's fire!"

(It's nice you're enjoying
what we're doin'
and it may be a little rad,
though it will never be good enough
saving your soul,
we're being up-front, telling you so)

(con't)

You're out there
you know who you are,
you get up after the music's over
headed for the nearest corridor
leaving out the side or
back door.

You refuse to believe
the message
you think it's just another line or raw deal,
but if you would pull over to the side
and stop for a moment
taking it in
your heart could feel God's love
trying to break through,
it is for real!

"While you're at the next concert
gettin' down on the sound,
remember if you wait too long
to make the change
you're rippin' yourself off
and it really is a crime;
you won't make that personal commitment
in time."

When you see the smoke surround you
know,
the flames aren't far behind.
"Where there's smoke there's fire!"

- - -

The Spirit Man
(within you)

Your eyes held the freedom
beauty
and promise of the lands
which your families lived and flourished
with the Great Spirit showing your hearts
in Thanksgiving, one for another.

"The white man destroyed your
hunting grounds
raped and slaughtered your women
and children
turned and crushed the spirit man within you,
suffering disgrace and heartbreak
forcing the remaining tribes onto sand dune reservations
was anything but honest."

All that's left is a handout from the
welfare department
comforting you with the white man's poisoned
fire water
numbing the pain of yesterday's nightmare,
caused with hatred, lies and
broken treaties.

Every proud chief dreams in hopes
of a strong righteous son
who would walk by his side
showing him everything the Great Spirit
has given him,
keeping his tribe in harmony
with earth's surrounding bounty.

Don't despair my red brother
hold up your head with
honor,
for the Great Spirit and His Son are returning

(con't)

to give back what's rightfully
yours,
make no mistake about it!

I've poured out my tears and
spirit
for what the blue coats did to you,
though the sorrow was brought upon your race
many moons ago before I came
being helpless now to free you;
the highest council has
spoken
and the spirit man will wear your war paint
into battle.

A great cloud will appear in the sky
and every eye will see
the Great Spirit's Son,
a warrior of awesome strength and power
whose name is Jesus Christ
returning your dreams,
sharing the lost homeland in
America and Canada.

"Though I'm only quarter blood
the spirit man flows through us
in visions,
speaking with a straight tongue.

When the hour comes rolling in
all those things your ancestors worked
so hard
to preserve for you,
will fill your hearts with peace an' love
once again"
- - -

Hell's Door

You can't see the way clear
yet you rant an' rave up and down
saying you can,
thinking after all these years
the story of Jesus told
hell is some kinda myth you'll never see,
if you don't invite the Good Shepherd in
setting yourself free.

You better fear God until He let's
you know
He's the God of love and discipline.
It isn't going to be
a weekend-picnic holiday you can handle,
thanks to your non-believing friends
who helped you reach there.

"Voicing secretly
it would be better without God
so we can do whatever we want
without any pay backs
is how it should be,
though you haven't a valid warrantee."

An example of a polluted brain
imprisoned,
doin' time for a horrible crime
convinced the devil will give his reward
when entering into hell's playground,
with a ten-thousand-piece band
welcoming him in,
singing: "Master, master, your every wish is our
command."

I hate to burst the dude's bubble
but somebody's got to tell him
how it's gonna be,

(con't)

and I pray you will take it in today and receive.

God doesn't care how tough you are,
when your ticket's punched
you're on the way down brother!

Your spirit will start breeding the
agonizing wounds an' open sores of grief
you inflicted on other innocent victims
with devastating pain so intense
the screams will be heard a long way away
for eternity!

It's a depth of scorching hot sorrow
through hell's door
one could never have dreamed possible,
stumbling, crawling around
thirsting for water,
being reminded endlessly why you're there!

People who don't believe in anything but science
and the material art of junk collecting feel,
"long as I pay my bills
take my prescription pills
wave to the neighbor across the hall or street
once a year,
trying not to swear
when feeling a moment of despair
is all I was brought up believing, life should be."

If by chance there is a heaven,
I'll make it upstairs when I leave
because there's no way someone like me
could get deceived.

It hurts having to explain this to ya,
"but life is a little bit deeper
than a millimeter on a ruler
or being
Mr. and Mrs. Goodie Two Shoes.
The bottom line is:
accepting Jesus into your heart
or meet the devil in the dark!"

- - -

You've Got To Do Good
(it's the only way up an outa' here)

You want everything
to go your way,
or you will freak out
'til you feel you've won.
In this world
no one gets his cake
and eats it too
like you think you're gonna do.
(You will pay for it in the long run)

Being lazy, prejudiced
with little direction
is no way to be,
spending time
going out of your mind
trying to look so fine,
what about the inside of you?

What good is growing old, suffering
"killing our future
doing only what you want
when you decide to do it,
is why we can't see the light of day
living to forget the past
leaving all you've heard and felt is true,"
think about it
what's the matter with you?
(You will pay for it in the long run)

The good spirit has to gain an entrance
in,
you can see through your own heart of hearts
God's showing you how to win.
"We're all carrying sicknesses
you've got to learn what they are
healing most of those scars

(con't)

116

will keep us from falling apart."

We're not giving up on faith
at any cost
while we wait for God and Jesus
to show us the way up an outa' here,
but you must have faith in hope
before you go.

"Find spiritual truth within
and live it
instead of walking around with
square blank heads,
thinking you're so super jive-time cool!"
Don't let me hear later
someone say
he or she didn't know what was
happening.
(You will pay for it in the long run)

Go into the world and look around
getting involved,
expand your horizons
there's much to be found
and done.

Plan ahead before it's
too late,
the evil that's being held in check
by God
will be released even more with every
passing year to date,
while the ugly one continues
to steal
your sacred fate

- - -

We're Going Home
(finally)

Before the rapture gathers
the flock together,
you'd think after working in this world
how long it's been
it may just take forever
before we learn what it is we're supposed
to do,
(for only a broken vessel
can help another through)

"If the Lord left it up to you
is why we're not free,
as everyone with authority enforces
on us
his own will
of how life should be,
when they don't even know themselves."

There is a dark force outside your door
ruthless and filled with despair
knowing his hour is almost here,
"causing our dreams to come up empty
when ever we choose to
grow-up;
teaching the bad attitudes
if it doesn't concern me then I
don't care."

I see the downfall of many
who wouldn't listen,
programmed for dirty movies
dream'n about kissin'.
While the spell lingers
again you grab for it with never
a doubt,
as nothing can ever shine

(con't)

117

because everybody figures he's got
the time,
but time is running out.

"Through what's being channeled into your head
you think you know what's going on
yet there's only one truth,
doing what's righteous
or ripping yourself and other people off;
trying to be a success
the world slips deeper and deeper
into his designed mess,
keeping them free to plunder God's values
without reaching their firey rest!"

(It's not going to keep taking forever
this is it, it's goin' down now
and we're really trying desperately
to find all the pieces
getting everything together,
so we can pull out
of this unforseeable weather)

There are people chosen
given truth to share
holding the ability of knowing what's
out there.

The first of many generations
now, "the very last,"
after the resurrection from Israel's land
the children lived out their lives
hoping it was them receiving the main promise
from within God's green left hand.

Time is close according to His will,
so let's pitch in and don't be still.
We must push back those fears
help carry that burden
and when the smoke clears,
we will find our way back to the land
of
milk and honey
- - -

I'd Do Anything For You, Girl

There are those times
when I feel what I feel for you,
and would undertake whatever I had to do
so I could be there with you,
after it was all said and done.

If a thunderstorm came upon me
while searching for you
feeling the rain run through
soaking my soul, thinking about you,
hope'n it would keep me free
from a fever or cold taking hold.

If I wandered into a blistering desert sun
thirsting for a drink of water
fighting through a sand storm,   thinking
"Is there such a girl like you?
I'd find a way, being in your laughter and fun.

If I were caught up in a winter's blizzard
trudging through snowdrifts
frozen to the bone and about to quit,
hoping there might be a possibility
you were real, an' you loved me,
gee whiz woman, I'd be there like that quick.

To reach you girl on that special day
our eyes meet for the first time,
"feeling each other's warmth of heart draw us
I'd be lost for words to say,
with that pounding feeling of nerves
comin' over me
as I see you step forward
in my direction."

Clinging to one another's hand
while soaring through the heavens above,
realizing our dreams will bridge forever, loves span
- - -

Our Wishes Of Worth

Throughout this world
we're always wishing,
wanting everything to shine
on us,
while so many
have little or nothing.
We must learn that worth
is in giving to someone,
not receiving for ourselves.
"If it's not turned around
we will drown
in our wishes of worth"
- - -

Iron Rod

The truth is within your reach people
those longing for
happiness,
first though,   separation of the weeds
from the wheat.

Years have come and gone
you've heard it in a trillion songs,
the population escalating into a
mighty throng,
every soul going a different way
refusing the Word of God
falling into decay.

"No, you don't want to listen
no, you don't want to do what's right,
you're big an' bad
you're out there on your own
and nobody can tell ya nothin'
because you know everything;
but little you know
it's God
runnin' the show!"

Stand if you can,
fixing your wicked eyes and cold heart
on the Holy One of Israel
when He's hitting you upside your head,
like an explosion from the
iron rod!

Jesus will uphold all things
in whatever His Father sees fit
crushing the rebellion of non-believers,
craving lust, perversion, over love
in their hearts
they know it's wrong,

(con't)

reaping the scorpion's sting.
You're gonna get your fair chance people
it will be up to you,
we're up here layin' this on ya
so you can make your way through
or face the tempered edge of the
iron rod.

Leaving the wake of corruption behind
one hopes to remember
during the millennium reign
why God has detained
putting aside man's evil
tempted ways.

"Before Satan is released again for a
short while
as every heart will try to maintain
without becoming vile,
but woe be to you the non-child,
during the last of the
last days."

The serpent of old, his cunning deceit
will strike the heart
with full fury blows
shaking our faith foundation,
lest we forget to magnify the Father and Son
within our soul.

Yes,
you who walk away
from God's given truth and grace,
will forfeit your right to life
during the
Great White Throne Judgement Seat
of the
Holy Lamb of God.

Peace and wisdom from on high
flowing through Jerusalem
keeping the home fire burning,
though many of the multitude refusing

(con't)

the righteous way
turning into evil during those awful days.

Satan plots to destroy
the Son
in the dark overcast gripping hour,
"yet His Father cometh quickly
from above
wielding the absolute almighty power,
placing His authority forever more
in Jesus' right hand
who spares not, the iron rod!"

If you look closely
with your ever-straining eye,
you may catch a glimpse of
what's held within the Son's right hand
that always survives,
used to destroy His enemies
they'll taste the dust of the earth's floor
once they hit it!

All glory and honor
of His will,
which He spoke thousands of years ago
from His holy hill,
rightly belongs to our loving
Father,
who constantly tests the steel
of the One who holds the
iron rod

- - -

Throw Away Children

When you're young and learning
to share
it seems so hard to do,
giving your parent or parents
fits
beyond reason
with lots of gray hair.

Becoming a teenager
still
you never learned to give too much
just receive,
and the affection you force
at a costly price
playing one against the other
like the adults love to do,
you know it's not right.

You're older now
and your children are the same
as you were;
some things never change.
The world being what it is
you're never around too much,
your son, daughter or baby sitter's
doin' your job
as everything seems to lose its worth somehow.

"Having no moral values instilled
the children feel pressured
when finding themselves in a heavy jam,
thinking there's no way out
no one to turn to,
the silent treatment is all you
ever gave
until you wanted your own way,
ya don't have much of a plan."

(con't)

121

Alcohol and drugs decrease your smarts
keeping you hooked
the children are led believing,
death over life
will set the hurt free,
because they couldn't identify with
a virtuous right,
destroying their precious inner light.

People in control
add up the tragedies as a whole
shaking their heads in despair
wondering what to do;
they can't seem to break through
the mainstream of sorrow
while pushing their own children away today
and again tomorrow.

"I'm not gonna let ya keep dragging
the children down.
You know damn well it's true
you've been teaching and believing
the material side of things
molding us like new little zombies,
is why we don't want nothin' to do
with you!"

We're all grown up
those of us that were able to make it
through,
now many of us have become worse off
than you!

"With T.V.
the throw away children
looking on,
you sit at your plush gatherings
in suit and tie,
coming off in all your wisdom
suppressing the lies,
the damage mounting
our children discarded,

(con't)

barely alive
livin' outside in somebody's garbage!"

You've called in your favors
getting to the front of the class
you want for nothing,
except true vision in the heart
is why this world needs a jump start.

Everywhere you turn
unsanctified people making babies
left and right,
knee deep in constant strife.
The guilty stain
you try removing as you debate
it's getting late,
watching our children's future
go down the drain!

"Being young and searching
they feed you nothing
spiritual,
in high school or college they outlaw it.
Later
you're on the street with no hope
always busy
looking for a half a pint, a bottle of wine
or a little dope,"
while people wondering if it's really true
all this fuss lately about Jesus.

Our Lord is close
the hour near
and when He comes crashing in on the
wicked,
backsliders too
during that dreadful day;
it's all gonna stop with your turn
to rot,
for throwing His Father's children   away!
- - -

Be A Giver, Not A Taker

In this world of give and take
the unsaved soul
takes ten times more,
than he gives.
You think it's just a coincidence
or another phase you're going through
when someone tries to help you see
the spiritual side.

"You shrug it off while
walking away,
it happens again and again
until the Lord gets through
saving ya anyway, if you're on His list."

You don't want to admit
there might be something to all
this,
because you would have to start
giving
for once in your life,
crying when having to part with those
green krinkles, (the almighty dollar)

Realize people, it's true
there's saved Christians
doin' it too
isn't it you,
singing your little hearts out
with song and praise,
until the shingles start popping off
the roof tops.

"When it's time to leave your place
of worship
supposedly to care for your neighbor
who's in need,

(con't)

your ungrateful heart turns
to greed!"

The evil in this world
is spreading like cancer
and we must be made aware,
doing what's right.

"The sinner looks at what the
Christian does
and sees the difference if he's
searching for truth
he will find his God in Jesus
and the closeness thereof,
changing
not making the same mistakes
a dozen times over an over."

The Christian that knows better
and we do,
but lives not the life
I think you should know,
all your singing and carrying on
in the name of Jesus
isn't worth doodlysquat
in our Lord's eyes
- - -

The Verdict

Though he is not against himself
nor is he for
himself,
yet being measured
by many
causing uncertainty that will not cease
within his soul,
"until truth
perfection and love
are forged between heaven and earth,
overcoming release of our
eternal bondage."

What may the reasons be
as you saw him
in the manner you did,
was his dream of being something
close to good, devoted
to the One who knows what goodness
is all about.

When the trial is completed
and he is found to be
innocent,
may he know freedom of a
different kind.

"People love to condemn
one another
without knowing the heart
as they expend all their energy
running the tongue ragged,"
is why our focus is far removed
from the mind's eye
while we're passing through this crazy trip,
called life

- - -

Eternally Shocked

You're fighting hard for all the wrong
reasons,
gaining those material possessions
listening to that sinister voice
inside your head,
thinking how comfortable you're gonna be
one day,
when you've got it all.

You decided to take it upon yourself
because you couldn't tolerate
couldn't change their faith fast enough,
so you slaughtered your fill
taking over their lands
calling it ethnic cleansing,
and right in my God's eyes to rape
and murder
destroying His people!

"When the living God
pours out His wrath on the unbelieving
blood-thirsty wicked,
the earth hardly holding together
you will find out then
you can't continue to believe
in yourself
and practice hating your neighbor
will keep you into the dark,"
is why you do what you do immorally
and you know it's wrong!

"Because of your own sick, ruthless
actions,
those who live by the sword shall die
by the sword,"
facing your eternal
downfall
reaping what you have sown,   forever!
- - -

124

Healing The Wounds

When you're growing up in any
city
and no one is around too much
showing you what's right or wrong,
the surroundings start looking real good
to ya.

"Drugs, gang operations, guns,
prostitution;
man, the sky's the limit
in the quick money fix you don't want to
resist."
Sooner or later things
turn bad.
Who can you depend on now
that you've been hit?
Your life's on the line
and it's taken a sudden twist.

If Mom and Dad aren't doing
what's right
or anyone else in your family,
your friends
running the streets
lying, stealing, mugging, raping and killing
your brothers and sisters,
an' this is all you know, that's real!

You must understand there's more to life
than getting even,
getting over on somebody else
because of what they may or may not
have done to ya,
or someone inside the family circle.

Once they're gone
you know you can't bring 'em back,

(con't)

so whatever might have been for them
their spoken thoughts an' dreams
to you,
weave it into what you want to do.
And in the end
it all won't be for nothing.

(You must search into your brokenness
and pain
realizing there's only one way
healing the abandonment, the rejection
in sorrow you're feeling,
because of what you have
lost,
or what someone has put you through
personally)

"It is the spiritual side of
God and Christ
waiting for you to bring it to mind,
shaking yourself loose
from the every day grind!,
leading up to death's row if you won't receive
the sign."

Let go of the old attitude
and believe there's a better way
solving those problems with your heart
and mind,
letting the hatred out
that's eating away the life in your
soul,
costing us valuable people and time.

Can't you feel it
growing up just to die
it's nothin' but a big fat lie,
because the evil spirits don't want to lose control
inside;
due to the disheartening conditions you were
raised,
within the concrete city
of graffiti,   blood and tears
- - -

The Revival Song

Hello out there, are you listening?
Tell us if you're ready to rock.
Are you pumped up to roll?
Well all right now, that's what we wanted to hear.
Yeah, the Lord has mercy on us blues
and rock n' rollers out there
cause we love to go get it, people.

Don't worry, we're not gonna lift ya up
to let ya down,
delivering a revival message
spreading the love of God all around.

"We've all traveled a long, long way
you're here now and we want ya to stay,
so please don't turn an'
walk, walk, walk away."

I know you've got something to say
as well
and we wish you could be up here
sharing it with everyone,
because we've all got some wild stories
to tell.
Let's keep our common goal
showing those searching the difference,
between heaven and hell.

"The unsaved brother who's blind
can't see the forest for the trees;
it's killing me to think
your old friends and mine too,
thinking we're the crazy converted Christians
that have lost our minds."

They're many people out there
who have been deeply hurt or disappointed

(con't)

in one way or another,
now they don't care.
We wait a life time for that special
hopeful day,
seeing our family and friends come around
into salvation.

What happens when someone almost accepts
the change,
"old skunk breath steps in at the last second
before they decide to get things right,
adding another link on the chain!"
This world
growing really really strange,
if we don't stay focused
we will never see home on the range.

Fighting to overcome
those who stand fast and believe,
the elect will do everything within their power
so you don't get deceived.

"We've traveled a long, long way
you're here now and we want ya to stay,
so please don't turn an'
walk, walk, walk away."

Wait on Jesus
He will bring the chosen through
to a higher level, a happier time
than what they're use to.
I said He will set
I said He will set
if you give Him a chance,
if you're seeking with all your
heart and soul
nothing evil could ever take and keep control!

"Just let Him find ya
let Him save ya
let Him heal ya,
let Him love ya
and set your soul free"
- - -

Youth Of Today

Everywhere you go,
to a mall
on a beach, at a concert,
a party or school,
you see the youth trying to look
a little bit different
in every kinda way;
made me think about Jesus
yesterday.

The example of outward appearance
He set,
very few children
saved or otherwise, follow today.

We need to do a little more than
talk about
how much we love the Lord
or acknowledge Him in our heads
only,
while pretending to live the life
in our hearts.
"If you saw His face in any
picture,
looking into His eyes
you could feel your heart screaming back
at ya,
walk in His likeness!"

Jesus never dyed His hair two or three
different colors
or shaved His head in sections.
He never wore earrings all over
His ears
through His nose, His lips,
or stuck safety pins up into His eyebrows.
He never tauted His body

(con't)

127

like a road map
to make Himself look like Joe Cool.

"Realize brothers an' sisters
it's the evil one
who's making you do these things,
and he doesn't care how insane looking
you make yourself up
to be;"
(you should see what
sin
has done to his face for eternity!)

If you searched deeper into your
heart and soul
you would understand for real
your face and body
is more than something you see
or feel,
I know you know.
Don't let the world's fashion trip
pressure you
into becoming a freak show.

You weren't born that way
so do what ya want
to do,
but look through our Master's eyes
and get the right view,
making room
for your family and friends to say:
"Hey,
you sure look a lot like Christ today"
- - -

The Soul's Journey

Darkness comes quickly
upon the soul,
with no time left to think
or say,
the next split second you're gone
and on your way.

"Once inside the darkness
I can't find you
Jesus,
but you know where my
soul lies.
I'm asking ya to reach out
for me
before, and after I die."

Bring me home through the darkness
Lord
if it has to be.
I don't much care   no more
long as I get there,
it will be good enough for me.

I tried to tell you Lord
in my own little way when I was alive
family and friends too,
though very few listened or understood
I never could figure out why.

Seems like no one cares enough to look
into this universal plan,
the big picture
called:
"We've gotta' reach the spiritual side
to survive,
for the life of me Jesus,   you know
I've tried."

(con't)

No,
many people don't know how we came
to be
in this world,
though they give their version
or two.

Yes it's true,
we don't know how or when
we're leaving
before we're through,
prior to finding answers to all our questions.

"If you've been good doing all
you could
then unexpectedly you're gone,
there's never enough grievin'
whatever the reason."

No man's an island people
there's only One
who is,
and if you want to go up there
from here,
"your Father in heaven has already sent
His living seal
postmark guaranteed,
that mankind would hopefully
see
before your soul's life-force
begins to flee"
- - -

On The Road

I know you're on the road
and it's lonely out there,
but your Brother's spirit is with you
what little you can feel Him
from time to time.

The mission I've sent you on
you know it's right.
If you humble yourself and pray
my Son will make ya feel good
all the time,
not just when you play,
(though even then,   sometimes
you're miles away, one from another)

"We're bringing the children to
realize,
when they see or hear
their favorite band make a stand
they belong to another world;
it's coming soon
as you point the way."

If the children listened to the lyrics
of your songs,
it would keep them from doing a lot
of wrong.

"Loneliness
is a cold empty, feelin, deep inside
we carry around with little
relief
when we're all alone,
until it gets so bad
we break down and cry;
many times we don't even know
why."

(con't)

"The longer we're on the road
the tougher it is to push away
the heartache,
trying to recall the love you feel
you're losing."

Your families, churches and friends
keep the fire of life burning
awaiting your return,
sharing with you all those changes
through love
since you've been gone.

The children grow and understand
the reason why
"as you look around and begin to see
your reward
and the children, their's;
seems like it's taking forever."

You poured it out, now you can take it in
feeling like brand new
because of what we do;
you are special indeed,   my selected few

- - -

Touch Us Father

If you know about God and His Word
it's because He's made you
aware.
"He's calling His children home
through something you can feel
inside,
yet few will be chosen
because of unbelief and the lack of love.
Believe, just believe
receiving His faith from a touch of grace."

Walk in guidance with Jesus and the
Holy Spirit
who teaches us the eternal way,
being looked upon and blessed because
we try
through God's brown eyes;
so don't delay.

You are the Holiest seed Father
there is no other,
the main stay
sharing with Your Son,
He brings us up an out into salvation
every day.

"The Christian flock is in agreement
Lord God,
for only You know the way to our freedom:
the light that carries us out of sight."

Children, children,
all this suffering isn't in vain
but our gain.
It's hell in many ways, though remember
the rapture's near and it's right,
so take heart;
we could be leaving here tonight
- - -

Heavenly Angels Of Light

When I'm outside looking skyward
Lord God,
You reveal Your angels
descending and ascending
all around me.

It's a breath-taking
sight
wondering who they are,
and what they do
for You,
while they float about with such
ease and grace.

"Often I think about getting up there
one day,
walking over to my stored treasure
sitting on it saying:
Yeah,
this is mine
and everything around me" (smile)
- - -

A World Of Sorrow

I've seen people come
and go,
I've seen their hurts and struggles
grow and grow
to my dismay,
I'm standing here crying inside
with little to say.

"I felt their broken souls even more
as I walk by
smelling the stench of death
hovering in the air,
with tears dripping off their faces
until I had to go;
how could anyone not care."

There's too many people and very little means
I have
to make a dent in what has to be mended.
The world really is beginning
to crumble apart,
taking with it the pure
and most sinister of hearts.

"Where ever you travel in the world
searching for truth and righteousness
is our hope,
that this sorrow will be brought
to an end,
though you turn around
it starts up some place else, all over again."

Raising up people
caring and loving for one another
their neighbor too
we must learn to do,
while those who know bring freedom
to a forgotten man,   and his motherland
- - -

We're Thankful

You've blessed me Father
giving visions
which concern the flock,
the seven brothers involved in one
know now
we're all a part of the same rock."

The world wishes and longs to see
these spiritual things
that passed through this generation,
though many have not seen them.
There is a day coming
the sheep will surely see
being fulfilled,
with your truth, love and mercy Lord God.

"I thank You for the
twenty-four elders
who sit in your administration near You
Father
in all their given wisdom,
especially the twelve Jewish apostles
You hand picked for Jesus,
helping us
through the coming millennial reign."

When our journey comes to the end
of another era,
"we will always have You
Father
Lord Jesus, the Holy Spirit
one another,
finding our way through
making home
where there are many grateful hearts
reflecting our eternal lasting love, of You"

- - -

The Unbelieving Parent

When the rapture comes
to the faithful
it will be a welcomed sight
for sore eyes.
The wicked man and woman will be
in utter shock and disbelief,
even more so
being totally angered
beyond relief.

There will be nothing you can do
to prevent it
except turn your life over to
Jesus
being saved,
otherwise suffer the cost!

"You've lived your life to the
fullest
without any guidelines,
you were an island
and would not submit to the truth,
the authority of
Jesus Christ.

You didn't believe what you heard
about the Word,
if you did,   you didn't care.
It meant nothing to you
holding little or no value."

You were determined to gain everything
for yourself,
made your own rules as you saw fit
you didn't need anybody,
one day
hoping to shine like the stars in the heavens

(con't)

making sure people looked up to you
where ever you went,
taking what you could get
without having any regrets!

Now feel the wrath of discipline
fall on you
like an earthquake!
What you hold dearest will be
uprooted
because you believed not
an' you never did anything for me.

You can hold onto or tie
your children
to your back in a knapsack;
your children will be taken away
from you,
because you have forsaken Me!
You will know then
I am
the Lord God Almighty
- - -

Reach The Other Side

The years have passed me by
being a non-believer,
confused about those who were
and bored out of my mind,
it's a possibility I've been wasting my time.

"I never wanted to relate too much with anything
close to good
never figured out why I should,
never wanted to do what I was told
never knew I had a soul."

A failure in many respects
finding it easier to
look the other way, lie and hide the truth.

The only thing I ever understood about life was
you start out young
then you grow old;   after that
nobody I ever talked with seemed to know.

"I never tried hard enough to reach inside
my heart,
for the life of me I didn't realize
that's where ya start.
Always thinking there would be time later
for all that Godly stuff
so what's the big rush,
doing what we learn is right
or lose
God's love and trust."

Finding this great world in despair
made my insides shake,
feeling the pain and sorrow collapse the barrier
I built around myself
because I didn't understand why I should care

(con't)

until it started to affect me
was I able to see I was nothing but a fake,
so I finally became aware.

Hopefully by the year 2007, or less
believe what you want
we're in the last days of Satin's maze,
where the light and muscle of the Trinity's power
will be all over us
like someone taking a hot steamy shower.

"With unrighteous people being left
paying the toll,
caught up in a new age cult taking the stroll.
Worshiping idols, demonic spirits
thinking it will show them a better way,
instead of praying to Christ
through their disenchanted soul."

Don't put this off
you won't want to endure the cost
of the seven-year tribulation
and it's not my imagination,
it's being handed down from the big Boss.

My heart goes out to ya to hide
and keep tight
if you miss the flight out;
God will take care of His own
once you have a change in heart.

Our people, self destructing more and more every day
learning the hard way,
(so whatever its gonna be for you
don't give up the right to be free, eternally)

"Reach out and take Jesus' hand
before you get caught by those people
wearing the mark of the beast,
while living off the land.
If you lose your life, know Jesus
will give it back to you immediately after
the tribulation ends"

- - -

The Wrong Made Right

Injustices are world wide
high an' low, past and
yet to come.
My thoughts scream out
for truth,
hoping the children will hear
but my voice is imprisoned
and I can't speak a word.
In today's society, even if it wasn't
more than likely,
no one would hear me anyway.

I see the horrors the reporters bring
over the news
and I get a tiny idea
through my tears
Lord Jesus
what Israel had done to you,
"wanting desperately to forget
one of their own
is why there's going to be a remnant
from every country left
says our heavenly Father, that you can bet!"

The connection is real
between yesterday's pain and today's.
You can't keep walking
in a daze
telling your friends,
I've got a few bumps and bruises
but I'm okay;
besides
nothing bad has happened to me
so why pray.
We never get an answer
so I'll keep on my merry way
following the ceremonies and traditions

(con't)

of the world,
flunking the test until it's time to pay.

How can you deny the inward feeling
of love
which everyone has felt during this world's
generation,
coming from God through Christ
above.

"The Jewish people might say
what's all the fuss,
it may be what you Christians believe
but not us."

When God takes away the love potion
from this world,
man will become even more
wicked
then we already are.
It will be a sign to you, accepting
a measured truth,
and it won't be our brother Moses
or anyone else from the days of old
pulling us through,
except you know who.

"Until the world accepts Jesus as its
Lord and Savior
repenting of its sins,
everyone's suffering will continue
long into the darkest of days
ahead,
because a wrong has to be made
and will be made,   right"

- - -

Lies Are Like Dust
(it's everywhere)

Don't hang your head and roll
your eyes
giving me that pathetic sigh
when I'm talking to you,
look at me!
You've been lying all along
and it hurts,
you tell me one thing
later I find you've committed adultery.

"My feelings are on fire
you're nothing but a liar,
and I'm readin' you off!
You walk in here stylish
thinking a few right words and
that look
will change the fix you're in."

Maybe take control
because you've been on a roll
but inside you don't care
about me.
You don't care about a lot of things.
You take and take
and I'm tired of giving,
so take yourself outa' this place
and stick your feelings
where the sun don't shine baby!

You're two-faced,
our relationship is over
our vows destroyed forever.
Get out of my life
I'm setting myself free,
you're not really the reconciliation
I need.

(con't)

Lies are like dust
it's everywhere.
I'm not going to let it be a part
of my life;
I'm not perfect, just real.
You can talk until you're blue
in the face
soon there won't be a trace,
this time I'm not listening.

"You're just another sick-o
with no moral fiber
trying to have it both ways.
I can't believe after all
this time
the chances I've given you,
you wouldn't change."

Some things I could overlook
though it's taken so long
to catch on
hoping you would do right
by me,
but enough is enough
there's no more love or trust.

You're nothing but a
low life
two timin' loser,
so pack your bags honey
and I'm not even being funny!
- - -

Foolish Pride

I've been trying to find a way
to tell you all these years
what you've made me feel like inside,
but I was so wrapped up
into me
I came and went like the tide.

"Now you're gone
I'm sitting here hurtin'
all alone,
wondering why it took me so long
to feel the real meaning
of the blues
through the love of you."

Playing the music for me
my whole life
never realizing the gift you've
given me Lord,
was because of You
for those around me.

I always thought it came from me
me,
I put in the time
taught myself what I wanted
to do.
No one could ever convince me
of playing the fool
thinking those ideas weren't mine,
man, I've messed up big time.

"I've come to the end of the line
my creativity has faded,
my hands and energy are slower
than they used to be.
I can sense there's something more

(con't)

138

going on here spiritually
than just me."

I look beyond the darkness
Lord Jesus
that tried sealing up my eyes,
hardening my soul which took
it's toll,
laughing at the truth
feeling his fiery darts
through a demonic heart,
when I knew it was wrong to play along
with foolish pride.

My friend's gone.
I loved him so much,
how can I tell him now where I
went wrong.
I play the blues in Your honor
Lord
it's what I love to do
while I think about You,
paying the ultimate price.

"The rejection, the betrayal, the humiliation
the brutal beatings, the crucifixion,
then Your life."

(It would serve me well to remember
others too,
the life an' love that we love
which was taken away from Him
in all His innocence
for someone like me, to be set free)

It's more than I can bear
as I look back
when the Holy Ghost is falling down
on me;
I know now,   when your life is gone
and you're not real,
it's really gone
- - -

Picking up the Pieces

Carrying their broken pieces of life
around
bitter, cold,
never willing to give them up
telling anyone who discovers;
the suffering being too deep to let go
or they don't know how.
The healer says it's never
too late
and you should start right now.

Knowing the truth and power
of you Lord
forgiving those who were
untrue,
so why is it so hard for us
to do?

"We can't ever heal
until we forgive those who trespass against
us
that's the deal.
Our Father would in turn and heal you
for real."

People are reaching out in
secret
to one they feel will listen,
for only another broken vessel senses
an' knows what to do
being through many kinds of heartache too.

If there is no pain
there's very little gain,
as it teaches us about ourselves
through another's character,
whether we like it or not.

(con't)

If I could take your grief
adding to my own
making it better for you
it's what I'd do;
before the evil side destroys another piece
of your broken heart
keeping you from reaching through.

I owe it to myself seeking
a way
letting the Lord show me how,
I'd like for you to hand over your sorrows
to Him now.

Happiness is what you will receive
feeling good again
laughing like you used to laugh,
feeling aloft
in that highest place of joy.

The written word is a powerful tool
from anyone's hand
the Lord using whoever He can
melting down the years of built-up ice,
(caused by those demons running in circles
fearing exposure to the light
like gamblers ruining their life!)

"Your spiritual growth
without Jesus
taking those hurts away
will cause your walk to have a slight decay,
so forgive
picking up the pieces
and find your way."

Our heavenly Father isn't playing
the fool.
He doesn't want you to think
He's being cruel,
but there is one very important thing left
you've got to do
- - -

Father

Oh Father, Father,
what else could I have said or done
for You
my heavenly Lord?
I see the faces of Your
children,
many having no idea
what's going to happen to them
if they won't take the time to look
for You.

I've done everything humanly possible
what little it may have been,
showing the children
Your truth today,
hoping they would want to live
the real Christian way
turning them on to the light
of Your precious Son Jesus.

"My heart is heavy with sorrow
Father,
and yes, I love the music of the blues
and I'm guilty,"
but it's not just the music
no, no,
but this feelin' deep inside
which carries an answer of faith
for life,
the hard-core children reject
that's bringing me into this darkest night;
slowly killing their soul
because they won't believe
it's what's right.

"Without those believers
crossing over

(con't)

from death to life
Lord God,
I've,   I've failed You
the children,   myself too."

Sensing a change after all these years
I can smell it in the air
as I overlook Your kingdoms in my mind;
they must have been beautiful
way back when,
though today, there's nothing left
to any of them.

Your children are why
we labor
with blood, sweat and tears,
wanting to take flight from this
ungodly place
with no more confusion or fear.

"Seeking Your righteous ways
Father
we must do,
for Your commandments and decrees are clear.
You've made mention of this to every
generation before
though very few seem to hear."
Hope you're one of the ones
who does.

My thoughts racing ahead
like a wind-swept fire out of control
trying to hang onto my own
crazy soul,
goin' back to our roots
where we need to be,
wondering when the children will field
that homeward seed
to care
realizing their inner spirit of freedom,
or count their total despair!"

- - -

I'm Needin' You Too, Girl

During one early morning
hour
before the break of day,
through the darkness
sensing your loving way.

Hoping I was really with you
yeah with you,
feeling your hand in mine
it felt so warm and right at the time.

My deepest fear came over me
when our hands slipped
apart,
(I knew you were still there
because I could feel you touch
my thigh,
and for the longest moment, I thought
I had to try)

"As I was opening my eyes
to the rays of light
streaming into my room,
I slowly moved my hand from my side
to find yours,
but reality set in once again
and all I could do,   was cry a little more
inside"
- - -

A Simple Prayer

Lord Jesus, Father God
I'm dreaming the most wildest of dreams.
Hoping one day
I'll be able to hang out
with the both of You,
alongside Your family of starry hosts
if it's cool.

"I'm asking Ya to make sure
the devil
doesn't take me away
through the course of time
cause he's nothin' of mine,
before he's put where he's gonna
stay,
making me another of his fools
I pray"
- - -

Music's Gift

Giving back your love
I had to learn what it was,
fusing the power
into one
like welding two pieces of metal together,
showing the children and others
who play
today's the day.

I won't be ashamed to say
Christian music is here to stay,
listening to our tunes
while having some fun along the way.

Music has a price
like everything else in life that's nice.
My appeal goes out to the brothers
of blues and rock.
You better think about what you're
doing
instead of just playing the part.

"If all you want to do is
love yourself
seeing how fast you can play,
how dolled up you can look
geared for the show on the main stage,
an' nothin' you're doin', by breathing life into helping
a lost soul find his way,
then I don't really want to know   who you are."

It's always later you find
what you've worked hard for is gone
maybe even loved
if there is such a courtship,
while you wonder what went wrong.
Romancing the inner hope

(con't)

of love
once you see the truth
of the gift,
being able to undo what was done
given enough time, after reaching the sign.

"Feeling the depth of sorrow bleed
no Band-Aid can fix,
a change has to work its way out
within your heart
saving the need,
don't tell me you can't see
where I'm coming from, you've got to believe!"

"I never gave you any credit
or the right time of day Lord Jesus
I can't deny,
I wanted to do what I wanted to do
and I did it."

Looking back at what I've done
musically,
it's been wasted for things of
this world
living the blind lie,
nothing anyone will want to hear in the
future
is why I've got to turn it around
and try.

"Together we understand the instruments
we hear,
unlocking the sounds within our
celestial soul
to a deeper meaning of life's gifted melody's
one can appreciate.

Whether we're grovin' on the black gospel,
rockin' out
or playing those funky, down trodden
earthy blues,
it's sanctified, it's real
and carries the Lord's zeal"

- - -

Don't Make That Mistake

The dark side loves it
when they can rip your life
apart,
while this secret passion builds
a fire
in your heart little sister;
you won't admit
you're out of control
ready to throw away your love,
crushing the soul.

There's no way you can make it
through each day
carrying the attitude:
"It's my body
I'll give it to whom I want,
fulfilling my daily boring selfish
sinister desire
regardless of who I hurt."

Your parents, if any
did the best they could
setting the example,
living in a world with a dying virtue.
You're rebelling against everything
you know is real;
come on girl, dig deeper inside
how does it make you feel!

Hey, why not, everybody else's doin' it.
You want it now baby
ya can't wait,
ready to give it away
to anyone
who senses your inner most precious craving
of you,
as a result here you are

(con't)

on the verge of being immoral
thinking nothing of it,
doin' it too.
No please don't, don't do it girl.

He doesn't love ya
you're just somebody different
added to his collection,
"as he whispers softly what you long
to hear
it builds and builds
until the coast is clear;
you both get excited believing the lie
then all you know
is which way his blood's
starting to flow."

(You justify it like it's nobody's business
but your own,
later you're pregnant or broken hearted
he's left you alone
thinking you were just getting started;
yet the burden you caused
carries over in your dreamy state
because you were curious
and couldn't wait)

It's an easy cop-out when you become
lazy
with no spirit-filled guided direction,
dropping out of school
ya can't find a job
your family is supporting
the both of you,
or living off the welfare system.
Look,
I believe in you, I know you're no fool!

"Don't listen to the evil voice
coaxing you to be
untrue,
you must fight your emotions girl

(con't)

you can't repair the damage
once you follow through,
letting him destroy
the very special being
of a
grown-up girl like you."

There's so much more
ahead,
take your time until you know it's the
Lord God leading you,
and don't give way to something else
the other boys or girls
may have said.

Find the yield sign
stop at the stop sign,
give your family and friends who love ya
a chance to reach you;
they know a little more than you give them
credit for.

Later,
becoming a woman
getting past those teenage years
all those seductive lures
that caused your tears,
"you will know the force of love
for another
when it's delivered
through the highest power from above,
because you didn't throw away
the enchantment
the most vital part of life's purity
within you,
taking flight like the mourning dove"

- - -

Right On

Everyone wants to write
the words
that stand the test of time.

Hoping it might be
the ticket,
receiving love's full impact
needed,
(flying across the great void
flooding an unaware heart into seeing
the spiritual side,
making a brand new start)

"Somehow it's always the other guy
who writes
what we want to say,
guess it's God's perfect way."

I will write for you
and you will write for me,
seems like that's how it should be
- - -

The Dance Of Hate
(within the human race)

In the white people's world
the old days of slavery
was considered the humane thing to do
for a useless lot of people,
keeping a tight chain
around the black man's neck
while they let the dog run free.

Craving excitement
the white boss man having secret desires
sent his wife into town
invited mine in to fool around,
raping her again and again
there was nothing I could do about it.

Still not satisfied
seems like nobody ever gets their fill,
made my youngest daughter
crawl into bed
breaking her fragile life in two,
as the boss man came outside smiling
telling me how nice it was.
I thought to myself, this can't be happening.
No, there wasn't anything I could do.

"During that night
out on the back porch alone
my heart bleeding
gazing into a starlit sky,
everything looked to be okay up there.
My tears started flowing down so bad
I asked the good Lord why:
Yeah, you know I asked Him this question."

Thinking all hope was lost
until a little while later, I could swear

(con't)

I heard someone say,
"my son, I'm carrying your pain."

Here in America
we've made some proper strides
doing what's right,
though our prejudice has buried itself
deep inside the heart,
so when we're face to face
the wonderful things we love to say.
Then afterwards,
talking about one another like you don't
want to know!

I hear they're breaking up apartheid
in South Africa, I wish it were true,
becoming like America when they're all through.
Those poor excuses for white people continue
shooting their own down in the street,
beating them half to death on a whim
getting away with it like they used to do!

"Come on, you human race
where ya been.
Filled with an under lament of disgrace!
When will you tear down those barriers
building a moral home suited
for all races?
Becoming equally educated, finding a good job
worth everything in working together!"

Oh Africa,
there's been more blood spilled on your land
than rain
while many feel to embrace the stain.
With truth and vision you will prevail,
waiting for Jesus to break this
ungodly power.
"Let's pray Him down here again soon
making room here and there,
letting those hypocrites answer
for their inflicted sorrows and detestable upbringing
like a rampaging typhoon!"
- - -

Food For Thought

Woo-we, we're getting ready
to cook up something real appetizing
for ya.
Hope you're hungry for
God's Word
as we are in wanting to bring it
to you.

For those non-believers out there
it may be only the music
you love
is why you're here,
"just be open long enough
to find out God really does care
what state
your soul is in."

There is a method to this
madness
a plan for you and me,
which flows from the hand
of an all-knowing, exalted God.
Keep searching until you find
your place
then give Him the nod.

With the help of Jesus
we can serve you up two things,
the music that makes ya
feel good
and the truth about God's
Holy Word
that will keep you alive,
if you honestly want to survive.

"All people can't say their way
is what's right

(con't)

there's only one truth and one light.
The rest are living in a
pipe dream
causing different believers
to argue and fight,
resenting the known fact
they will find out
deep inside their inner core,
it's Jesus
who's dearest in God's sight."

Seek through prayer
the One who gives the song
that you've been feelin' off an on,
taking the answer back home
to those people who would welcome the delivery
with open arms,
whether you're from the city
or on a farm.

"Within the spiritual realm
of things to come
there is a delicious fulfilling
menu,
chasing away those mental and physical
hunger pains
through the hearts of God and Christ,
as you sense then reach for eternal life."

When you move forward admitting
you want to be a part
eating this celestial food
which was prepared for you,
in believing the message by not being fooled.

You're telling Jesus you want to be
trusted
digesting God's truth
learning a guided control
filling the void within your soul,
while enjoying the music we all love
to feel
it doesn't get any more real

- - -

Always In A Hurry
(to go steady)

It's You Lord God, it has to be.
I'm asking You to help me find
who it is,
help me understand
help me slow it down
before my heart crashes to the ground,
once again.

We try making things happen for ourselves
never waiting on You Lord.
Seeing what people do when they're fighting
brings a deep agonizing sigh.
"Its not what anyone should have to look forward to
in a relationship
when you profess love, one to another.
A little while later
you ignore, cheat, break up, or kill each other."

I've tried weighing it out
I can't see where it's wrong
knowing we can make things right
with spiritual insight;
it's what everyone should value in life.

As I look ahead in time
wondering what part really exists under heaven
and why people struggle so hard to get
something going,
then afterwards quit, letting their true colors show.

"When you feel that sacred love
oozing up inside
you've got to keep it alive by pushing the drive,
yet one must be real enough seeing through
the evil veil, of lies.
Let it be that way for me
or keep me forever dreaming
until you set my weary soul, ascending freely"

- - -

148

Love's Way

Gracefully I kneel
in learned faith
knowing Jesus is the one.

"I look to You Lord,
searching for the one true
holy fountain of light
is our mission within the unsaved
children's sight."

I hear people say everywhere
I go
we long for You to come oh Father and Son
letting Your will be done.

We're tired of messing things up
feeling bad
when we try doing everything by ourselves.
We would rather You show us
so we could be happy and glad.

After these thousands of years
gone by
You're giving us back,   love's way
- - -

Communication Power

They're just words
people write and speak
everywhere we happen to be
so they can have something
to say,
but who's really listening
enough
to take it in anyway?

Don't tell me you might be
wanting to see,
why it's the in thing
for searching people like
you and me.

"Sense and feel the power
flowing through the
air,
filtering into your emotions with a certain
dramatic flair, if you dare."

It's the reason through every season
we express
how much we care about
one another,
trying to reach our sister an' brother.

"Getting together when we can
breaking down the barriers
of man,
pressing ever so gently
to identify
what we have in common,
sculpting the spiritual force
within us
is what we love, to do;
working hard to communicate
before it's too late"

- - -

Check It Out

You want to hear the song
of songs
you want to know where the
wind has gone,
you want to be what you dream to be
and if you reach there what will you see?

We have a world that's falling apart
a few saved people holding onto
a light in the dark,
the rebellious and wicked think it's a farce
the secret's kept until they accept their part,
take a closer look inside your heart of hearts!

The rain and sun soak our earth
bringing life
now turned to strife,
what's you're family doin' about it tonight?
There's too many women out of wedlock
giving birth
there's too many lost people
knocking the Christian church,
will you ever find your inner spirit worth?

"Us believers hold the key
through the power of Christ
unlocking the door,
soon those evil doers won't hurt us
no more."

You want to hear
you want to hear the song
of songs
we want to know where the truth
of morality has gone,
you love to dream every day of what could be
if you don't find Jesus
you will never be free, once you leave!

- - -

There Is An Answer

There is life
there is gentleness,
there is a contrite spirit, within you.

There is understanding
there is compassion
there is truth,
there is love that belongs to all.

"There is a God in heaven
there is His Son Jesus,
there is forgiveness for every kind of
sin;
there is hope once you believe."

There is a real home you may enter
after leaving this world
by refining the spirit man inside,
bringing us through those tough trials
we bear
if you would only seek the answer
that's there.

"For faith without works
produces a hollow tree,
don't let it end up being
you or me"

- - -

Touch Me Softly
(forever)

Searching through eternities'
realms
for what's right
through love's narrow path,
is what I bring to you.

"Wondering as I walk
away,
will you ever feel anything
to do
the love, I leave."

It's a very
special moment
reaching peoples' hearts.
Let it be real
let it remain, forever
- - -

Be Humble, Be Low

Take a deep breath and let it out slow
then humble thyself
or stay caught in the devil's den,
where all denial and pain
descends.

Let the truth be known
as it cuts through your flesh into the bone,
you've built up a chasm pushing me away
and left me standing here thinkin',
"how many years will it take before
the evil one
turns your warm heart to stone?"

The devil did his usual dirty work
building up your pride
and those special things I heard ya say
you were going do with me,
I looked around to find
you took the liberty choosing not to see.

Being unaware
you loved hearing yourself talk
his lies
you never bothered saying goodbye;
oh yes, you were filled up big time
with worldly pride.
It's too bad you couldn't receive through
humility's eyes.

"I think about this trust we try to share
when people first meet,
and later how it turns to rust
like the world being sprinkled daily
with dust
breaks another heart to bleed,
because spiritually you've yet to reach there."

(con't)

The chosen of God sense the world
changing its disguise
listening to His voice we rely,
the double minded man is in us all
if we don't cut it lose to that certain degree
will cause our fall.

Being bombarded by the devil's
demonic deeds
is how our heart an' spirit get affected
disregarding the need.

"Pushing humility away
ending up with just another reason
going your own way,
because you were too hard headed
to believe,
you're less one branch from God's
holy tree"

- - -

Welcome Home

A certain young boy in his teens
raised in a Christian home
figured he knew it all,
rebelled
and went out on his own.

He never really accepted Jesus into
his heart
just going to church, playing the part
which was evident when he took everything
belonging to him
given by his father,
and tried making a different start.

The years passed by
things weren't going all that great,
"one night fighting dire straights
realized the spiritual need of being
lost,
went back to church one evening during the
Lord's Supper
found his Mom an' Dad
and felt again the love he was missing;
flowing down from heaven above
was God's holy unconditional driving love."

While he sat next to his family
and best friend
he felt the conviction of the Holy Spirit
within,
"knew he didn't want to suffer
the cost
went forward at the end of the service
when the invitation was given,
reached out for Jesus
and found life's real meaning
inside the cross"

- - -

Somewhere In Between

What is it I feel so strong
inside
when I think about or see you?
I don't want it to be a lie
hiding our feelings
causing our spirits to wonder why.

What should be said and brought
into the light
ya know things have to be made right.

The grace of God knows where
we are
feeling love from you is one of the greatest parts,
breaking through the dark dominion
of the night
due to a beautiful heart.

You can learn from him and him
about you
your feelings never falling through
because you love Me so,
and what's left is for the both of you
to know.

Being refined through tough times
needing the love of you
to make a stand,
marriage first, that's the plan.

Your work together
can start to revise an age old-story
teaching my children
with your two hearts and Mine on demand,
enjoying the glory already in hand.

There is a way for the world to heal
finding answers you seek

(con't)

given only to the meek.

Keep your love anew like early
morning dew,
your spirits soaring aloft feeling alive
filled with laughter an' joy ya never have to hide.

Never forget where you came from
it's a vital part needed to breathe
if we're gonna work like the missionary
with a visionary soul,
look at the need around you
letting the work take hold
learning about your blessings bestowed.

"Sometimes life shows a certain
unexpected way
searching every avenue
to reach love's painless stay,
though it's brought in moments
we want it to last through each an' every day,
especially when we're away."

There's no competition out there
that could touch your delicate faith
or match your pretty face,
through hearts of heated warmth we embrace
praying it's right with no disgrace

- - -

Tears Inside The Dark

Tears crying in the dark
keep tearing me apart,   as it finds its mark
is why I feel the blues from a
broken heart,
makes me realize the evil side of things
in how it all starts.

Uncaring people professing their belief in
Christ
is what they say,
never changing their character
living the right kind of life
brings sorrow on us like a thief in the night!

By day's end we're hurting so bad
praying to fall asleep in our bed,
"the truth kept with faith in God
won't begin right away
there's little we can do until it does,
sends tears flowing down feeling the loss
revealing the deepest side of the valley
nobody wants to tread."

Jesus, we're waiting patiently for You
to do Your part
is why there's a sea of tears raining down
in the dark,
dreaming of Your love coming through
igniting the start,
we're tired seeing our friends walk around
with no inner vision and suffering hearts.

"We hold our hope alive in You, Lord
who can heal and restore the walls of a
rejected, dying heart,
yeah, those tears in the dark
keep tearing me apart,   as it finds its mark
yeah, tears inside the dark"

- - -

You're Killin' Me B

As the situation becomes more
difficult
in other countries to survive,
people struggle one way or another
reaching America,
embracing with both arms an' heart
wide open
this nation called freedom.

They set up their own little world
of ways and means
bringing with them their different insight,
cashing in those dollars and cents
rejecting everything else around them.

This dying freedom is almost spent
nobody can afford the skyrocketing rent,
crippling this over burdened country
which was paid for
by our founding Christian forefathers,
but we hold the trump of defense.

Because you have little or no moral
spiritual belief,
you're turning our country and others
like us
into another Sodom and Gomorrah.

So embrace also, the wrath of God
soon to come upon you,
as it's headed this way!

We've gone from strong work and moral
ethics
to partying all night long
lounging around all day,
collecting the welfare checks

(con't)

making more an' more babies,
"thinking, isn't life and love
just grand,
yeah, you know it goes hand in hand
in this beautiful land;
out of yours and into mine."

"The changes are coming down
and the welfare party is gonna stop
people,
enough is enough.
We've become in part
a nation of lazy good for nothin'
loafers,
(an' you know who you are!)

Nobody owes you nothing
unless you truly are in need,
then its understood.

Your immoral, slick fraudulent ways
is gonna cost you your
soul today,
unless you get it together spiritually
straightening out your foreplay,
because you're killin' me b
you're killin' me"

- - -

Waiting On You

Please Jesus
don't,
don't tarry too much longer brother
we need ya man.

It grieves my heart to no end Lord
for those people who believe
the world is going to take care of itself
because man has the brains to bring back
the garden
like it used to be, without You.

Little do they realize it's never gonna happen
as the sceptics will see.

I know You and your Father are real
in spirit.
I've waited my whole life for this moment
in time,
to behold something pure and holy
like You Lord.

You are the only living seal
Lucifer couldn't destroy.

"This generation will not pass away
until they witness the terrifying events
destined for the coming years,
being made to believe in the
One
they refuse to accept."

I've got to tell ya,
it's the best dream of all dreams come true
and it's here for you to,
because any good believer knows
nothing is gonna stop the power of our

(con't)

Father's will
once He starts to move through the
demonic wall;
you better pray you don't get caught
in the way.

Please people
don't,
don't tarry too much longer
because forever in darkness and pain
is a long time to spend, alone.

"You can laugh, deny and curse the truth
until your buldging eye balls pop outa' your face,
but sooner or later you will stand
before the Man,
answering for your lack of faith in His
only begotten Son,
as you start shaking uncontrollably with
disbelief
at the sentence of judgement flowing into your
wicked soul!"

You better dig a deeper grove inside
the heart
getting hip quick,
opening up your mind to the invisible fix
and check out the real God
of this world today
before life as you know it, gets taken away.

Please people
don't,
don't keep sitting on the fence
worshiping worldly idols,
lifeless pieces of glass, plastic, stone, wood
or parking meters,
they can't do nothin' for ya.

"The warnings are coming upon the earth
slow but sure
as nature takes its devastating course,

(con't)

you don't have to be a weatherman
to figure out the score,
nursing an incurable sore."

Please people
don't you,
don't you want to try and understand
the spirit is a happen thing,
or is it too much of a strain on your
tiny little brain,
figuring there's got to be `another way
avoiding eternal pain.

I don't want it to end up this way
for you
searching for the right words
being carried on the whirlwind,
reaching through finding you
is what I've got to do.

"By throwing away life's spiritual
saving force
staying deceived in the dark
is really missing the mark."

Examine the situation around you
and see if prayer to Christ
is right.
You will be answered by Him before you
lose heart,
learning the hidden secret
that's been near you from the very start.

Before the great delusion is cast upon
the earth
worshiping the imposter,
because you failed to listen to His servants
in caring about saving love.

Being blessed seeing the difference
is where its at;
trust me,   it's more than a dream
from God above
- - -

Lovin' You Wasn't Easy

Though we've known one another
all our lives
I thought lovin' you was easy,
realizing later
we would never make it
seeing you again was nice.
So I say goodbye to you
an' me
and we do it willingly;
I'm about as good for you baby
as you are for me.

Lovin' you was special
you're every woman I ever loved,
we're so much alike
yet so far apart
"like two hands in a glove."

We're both looking back
our lives changed,
thinking
"lovin' you wasn't so easy
even though I hoped we could
make it,
it really makes no sense
to put us through this whole thing
all over again."

Looking back
on everything girl,
I'd like to think the next time around
we would remember the right way
in love.
We should have known
we couldn't do it on our own
but oh, how everybody tries
until it falls apart

(con't)

destroying one another's
heart.
So I say goodbye to you
an' me
and we do it willingly;
"because I was as good for you baby
as you were for me"
- - -

An honorable mention written by Charlie Sherbert
with a little help from his friend. "I'll never forget ya man.
Hope to see u on the other side when I reach there."

An Afterword

The question is, what is it we're all looking for in this world? Truth, that's it. That's what it takes. The spiritual truth is what we must seek every day. "Proven through underhanded deeds, deterrence through spiritual temperance is your shield," for only a few walk in truth in brotherhood because unsaved people think there's everything to gain from this greedy material world down here. There was a brother who told me "the happy trees are green."I found later he wasn't talking about the trees in the front yard or nearest park, but it was of a spiritual nature, an inner color of a man's spirit, granted only to a few brothers. Yes, material things in life are a help to us sometimes, though how can we enjoy them knowing it's only a show, for many? People who have such luxuries which they plan to keep at any cost, know they can't take it with them when they leave, though they hardly ever share unless they see a way to gain from it.

May the goodness of creation be open to the unknowing and most importantly to the children who have heard the word and make a sincere effort to find what's been hidden from them in this outpouring of work. As the rapture draws near, people living for the party will find themselves left here awaiting the real party, and I don't think they will be enjoying the get down groove of the beat too much, when they see what's in store for them! Ever wonder why very few understand and where their thoughts lie when you're near, wishing you could get through the confusion, depression, the self-centered soaring ego, false passions which leaves ya empty afterwards, along with the material gimmies?

Realize the inner secret of people speaking about another's religion, where they're from, as well as the color of one's skin, like dirt! If man were so smart as he thinks he is, problems affecting our families' feelings, beliefs, and the hatred of one's looks wouldn't be! This just goes to show, no one anywhere is as intelligent as he or she may lead you to believe. Where is all this taking us, the hate, lying, abuse, adultery, living like slobs, greed for money and power that keep people weak, blind, unless they fight it? We all know how tough it is to admit we made a mistake to someone, never mind wanting to confess it to God, asking for forgiveness, but that's the real deal. If you want freedom for your family and friends tomorrow, take heed or pay for your wickedness and unbelief!

When all of this has been "taken in," maybe then one can know the spiritual truth and reach to give instead of scheming to take, making himself look good in plain view. Please don't get left behind because when push comes to shove, the bottom line is, if you do, you will realize it too late," though there will be one more chance for you to get it together. Don't let the devil fool you a second time because it will be too late for you then! It may seem crazy to ya, and your friends will probably have a good laugh, but you will see "this is as real as you are, if you really are

(S)

This isn't a game show or soap opera you've been watching on T.V. to entertain you all these years, it's about your future, now or never. You must be a soldier and I pray you will join God's army, because He's the real general of every battle you'll ever fight on mother earth. All we have left is right here now that God is letting man know about, so please seek the truth in time, as God will reveal it to you, before you "throw away your dreams, your world included."

There may be another sign given soon concerning the Ten Nation Common Market countries over in Europe. It is my hope God Almighty will show everyone this Major Bible Prophecy in that it will come to pass prior to the rapture of believers of Jesus Christ. You will know then <u>truthfully</u> "what is written in the Christian Word of God, is for real!" When you hear or see these events happen, know it was prophesied a long time ago by the "Jewish prophets" and you better make the attitude change quickly by "using the long jump method," accepting Jesus as your Lord and Savior (smile). When the Ten Nation Common Market countries hook up as one, realize in your heart, you can take it to the bank and it won't bounce, because the hour will be short for you in making up your mind! If all that is received by you falls on deaf ears because you refuse to believe and you miss the rapture, you will see the "world ruler or false prophet" come into power by taking over three of the ten European countries then the other seven. After that, there will be a seven year peace treaty drawn up with Israel which will be broken three and a half years later. At that point anybody with half a heart and a pea brain will know he's been had!

Okay, so you finally see clear now but you think there's no way out for you or your family and friends. You think to yourself, I'll just go with the flow, accept the mark of the beast on my hand, keep it in my pocket and everybody guessing. No, don't accept the mark on you. Accept the Lord Jesus into your heart and fight against everything that's wrong. Now that you realize the unjust ways of man, come on you've lived it, when things go wrong you hear yourself say in a moment of anger when it's directed at you, "if it isn't one thing, it's another!" When the shoe's on the other foot while traveling through life as things go smoothly for ya, is why one should think and be thankful for what he's got, though it's never enough. "Hint," your heart and soul, it's all you need man. Remember, don't leave home without it. (smile).

Don't lose sight doing the one or two things in life that get you by materially, because regardless of what you think you know, the only thing that matters, "is the salvation of your spirit and yep, you've got one in there, somewhere" (smile). If you won't humble yourself and pray in Jesus' name today, you're gonna be one sorry stressed-out dude on judgement day!

The Bible is the answer, there is none above it. Jesus Christ lives today and has but one given name from God Almighty. It was Jesus Christ 2000 years ago; it's still Jesus now and tomorrow.

Our Father waits patiently, high in the universe until He makes His move and it

(T)

will be soon. To the people covering this earth, they must realize that they can't live in a world with good and evil in it, and goodness will be the final result.

Remember it's God you must confess your sin to through His mediator Jesus Christ and those of you who think not, you're being deceived, because your sin is <u>not</u> forgiven. Jesus was the only Prophet who died for all our sin and no other human being on earth can claim that truth. He is the purity, our example.

For the majority of runaway denominations today, teaching just enough doctrine to call themselves a seeker of truth in Christ, yet they're on the edge of being a cult because they refuse to accept the truth from the scrolls Jesus Himself held and read in the synagogues many years ago. The first chosen Israelites of God shaped our world events then, and today, but it was not being done fairly by the Jews at that time, is why Jesus was sent by God to show the poor uneducated Jews and eventually the world, another way spiritually; in how our heavenly Father wanted things to be done. So here we are on the threshold, drawing closer to the year 2000, a new era of time unfolding before the world, while people are still unwilling to believe all of His Holy Word, professing to keep God's commandments and decrees, but don't.

Remember to keep the Sabbath, the Lord's Supper and the gathering of the saints for fellowship sacred, and you will be blessed by our Father.

I've tried to explain what's ahead of us as humanely and compassionately as I know how, and it is my hope you have learned "a little something spiritual." It is to your benefit breaking down the barriers we build around our feelings and thoughts that hide from us the truth we seek to know.

If you choose the present system, later the mark of the beast, as it will come to pass, and you repent not of your sins, I'll be signing you up for the "eternal burn unit" because you're gonna be busy 24 hours a day and you can count on being greeted in, rather warmly.

Finally, for all those Christians who used to be ablaze for God, though you have lost the fire and zeal somewhat, I hope this book has brought you back once again to deeper soil where you want to be, in all your hopes and dreams that are real. Try to understand it's taking a little more of God's time to work them through into your life, when you first realized the value of being saved through the spirit of our Lord Jesus. Please don't let the flame smolder and die out. Don't turn away once your feelings reveal to you this truth, because the rapture is coming and concerns those who truly want to travel on home to a better place, and happier times. Praise be to God and His only true Son, very few want to recognize until Armageddon opens up that blind spot of fog between their ears.

And so, as the real cartoon of cartoons go, "That, that, that's all folks." (smile).

May peace be with you on your journey, where you may hopefully find what's really happening on the inside, "and to the ones you say you love, on the outside." Are you ready to soar?

(U)
Have Reached
The End

"The rapture will separate
those who believe
from those who
think
they perceive,
what's right."

My Commentary:

I didn't write this book to shove religion down anyone's throat, and understand it's not religion I'm feeding ya but a personal relationship between you, Jesus, and God our Father. You have found I'm sure, many secular (meaning non-religious) writings as well, telling true stories of our world being brought to you on your own level. When I was in the world I too was lost before God touched my life and made me see His truth through the lies the evil side loves to spread. The mission today is still salvation for the unknowing, or ungodly person who thinks he's an island and holds the power of life in his own hand. Though it's the dark side who lets you think you're invincible until you believe it, but it couldn't be further from the truth. I'm trying to let you see there are more important things going on spiritually than meets the eye, your eyes. There is a spiritual key of life and it wasn't made by you or me. What's this all about? The truth for a change, creation's destined plan of a Divine Being who has made Himself felt to all peoples, you can't deny. The millennium is just ahead with time being short for deciding between the material idols we love an chase after, or will it be the "spiritual things of heaven, that are yet to be realized by you?" I don't care if you're a genius or if you're not. I don't care if you're a high school or university graduate. I don't care what country, reservation, town, or city you come from.

What I do care about is everyone's' feelings. It matters because it's all we have left to share and hold onto between one another, "through where we've been, where we are now, and where we will be headed later, if we don't start getting things together for real."

School is right and very much needed. While it teaches us the basic alphabet, numbers and science with a hope the student will excel one day, helping his society to survive. What high school and college doesn't teach you in the secular realm is why this book was written. It is our streets filled with blood, the broken homes, where the truth of sorrow in life dwells that the teachers and professors avoid teaching our children, who are hurting and searching for what's real on the inside of the heart and soul, "because this is, the way it is!"

The reason for this tragic shortcoming is very few people really know what it takes to relate spiritually, though they would if Christ were living in them.

People should take a good look outside their door or watch the news a little closer, they would see what man is doing to our families, in all their twisted wisdom turned to greed! It won't be anything man will do in bringing this world back together again, but the spiritual power of God and Christ is what we wait and long for, those who are hip to what's goin' down.

If you take the time to reach within yourself, (that's where it all starts) you will discover the answers to the severed cord of life, while traveling down this crazy road of ours.

Paul Eugene Barr

Pauly Boy